POETRY FROM BEYOND THE GRAVE.

this work is licensed under the creative commons
attribution-noncommercial-noderivs 3.0 unported license.
http://creativecommons.org/licenses/by-nc-nd/3.0/

originally published as *parnaso de além-túmulo*. portuguese version
publicly available at the *biblioteca virtual autores espíritas clássicos*:
http://www.autoresespiritasclassicos.com/

printed by lightning source, milton keynes
in an endless edition (version 131005)
ISBN 978-90-817091-9-4

uitgeverij, den haag
shtëpia botuese, tiranë
editora, campinas
出版社, singapore

www.uitgeverij.cc

FRANCISCO CÂNDIDO XAVIER,

Poetry from Beyond the Grave.

EDITED AND TRANSLATED BY
VITOR PEQUENO
WITH AN AFTERWORD BY
JEREMY FERNANDO.

:

Translator's Note

Something is always thought to be lost in translation. Something, singular. Something singular, you might say. Not particular expressions or words too dear to do away with, but more importantly a thing; a block-solid, sensible object in the world; the means through which one means to be among others. Matter is lost. Something with three dimensions, stretching out. Not meanings, but ink; not ideas, but material, organizing logics; not a generalizable sense, but a specific political position, of a specific timely – and mortal – subject. Even here, with Francisco Cândido, or Chico, Xavier. Maybe even specially here with him.

To translate has very much to do with poetry: it is an exercise of uncoupling signifiers from their chain, to search for, and force the limits of, different referential patterns. It has to deal with opening dossiers, as I'm sure Jeremy Fernando would like me to say, through different material means within the boundaries of language, as we remember, there are no traces outside them. One most often translates the words only because our words can be so similar to one another's in so many ways. But switching word registries is not the organizing principle of translating. Following logics and respecting positions is. In that process, one must discover what it is that one can do without; and what must remain even after all the heavy, three-dimensional weighty things that words can be, are gone.

That is why I find myself with the obligation of insisting that translators cannot apologize for losing something in translation: that is their office. To lose something; to let somebody go, to let that which cannot be reached around to, fall away. However, here, an apology is still owed to the reader. Not for the exercise of losing what it is the translator attempts to lose in order to find the text; but for the unlawful attempt to discover what it was that could still be found. Or gained. Or made here. I cannot take credit for a translation of this impressive work so much as for a reading of it, and as Fernando will trace out with much more skill later on, a reading is full of gestures: of interpretation, negotiation, forgetting, erasing. A palimpsest. It is my own personal attempt to make sense of it. It bears those marks. And I apologize.

What you are left with in the end are the very words Chico Xavier used, but built differently, inside different contexts, accomplishing different goals. I feel that these translations, for instance, bear less traces of the perfection implied by the rhyming scheme of the original text, the search for the absolutely perfect logic of the Creator; and a lot more to do with the experience of a dream, which follows its own proprietary logic, and spins only ever around the axis of language, and becoming.

We started with the ordinary problems of translating. First, we discovered coherence of terms to be an unrealistic goal: dozens of authors (and of course here, I don't necessarily mean different people, only at least, different discursive positions), and each with their own intentions, made standardizing attempts quickly become silly exercises, really. Each *Terra, Céu,*

Divindade, Pureza, came from somewhere. It became, rather plainly, something impossible to ignore. The first step we took then, was to translate each poem as if it were the only one that would be translated at all. We abandoned standardization, and met with each of them without plans.

The second question, and a major one, was regarding the rhyme scheme. To say this is no free verse poetry is (with a small grin) to say the least. Being entirely written on very well-measured metric structures, the poems give off the impression of being the mortar of the architectural foundations over which the Astral City itself is built: solid, peaceful, stony words in rich rhymes that seem to be the bulk of the meaning one gets from the poems, when read in Portuguese: it alludes to a perfect order and, right off the bat, it became stupendously hard to get across. But as any native reader will tell you when reading these poems, there is something much stranger and bewildering to the eye than the rhyme scheme used. The vocabulary is composed almost entirely of royal, antiquated, and just plain impossible terms, half of which any native speaker of the language has surely never heard before. The archaic phrasing of a rural world. And so it was that the first attempts at maintaining the structure and the lexicon were absolute failures.

In the progress of reading the text, though, something else, clearer and more profound, became apparent. Something lost somewhere in between the mighty pillars of perfect meter and perfect rhyme. Something that the words themselves revealed, we followed, and now must apologize for: it was a journey through limbo, the one Chico undertook. Whether you believe him or not (and we cannot pretend that believing him or not isn't relevant in the context of reading this), it was the journey required of him, to write his stories about journeys through dreams. To write about something that is lost, and the things that can be gained along that way. More than anything, it was important to find that, in his poetry. And that is my reading of it.

Understanding Brazilian Spiritism has a lot to do with understanding the three-dimensional things that made up life in rural Brazil at the turn of the twentieth century. Things I would scarcely understand myself. Third-world things like hunger: the pain and sadness of it; and toil in the form of aching backs and unschooled children; and the long dirt roads leading nowhere, never letting anyone around any words except their own. Things like the hardship of poverty as a helplessness and a bitterness, the fiery chasm of religious fervor and dogma; the scary pain of death manifested as buckets of tears, dishes from neighbors and absolutely nothing else: people that don't remain; bear the marks, but leave no traces. Lives that are that play out as something akin to the oldest country songs there are; the wondering lives of freed slaves in the south after the Civil War. Some kind of sadness. Brazil at the turn of the century would have housed few stories to surprise educated readers. It was the stage of small wars, but no genocides, small miracles, yet no salvation. It was a country of small towns and big churches, and in the middle of the infinite expanse of rural Minas Gerais, this boy, burdened by grief, death, and trauma, just started to write. Why and how he started to write we do not know. But the why and how he started to write couldn't matter all that much to us, is the truth. Belief is power here, and amidst all the lessons Chico took down from the dead, we can agree one he mastered was the secret of how to live forever. How ironic, how appropriate. One book can be many different things, it seems. And so this is my reading of it, and the where and why he wrote what he wrote as he did.

A whole century later, in a time of evidence and certainty, we hear a lot of the discourse of Spiritism here as being proof-centered. The sentences always end in something similar to "… how could he have known that if he wasn't…?" Of course, as any freshman philosophy student knows, some arguments are circular, the very words themselves bringing you back to the beginning. It is, quite elegantly, a question of faith: if you have it, then the question is answered. Following the same beat, we opted for a leap of faith in translating: we did away with rhyme, and away with the structure, and away with perfection. Got rid of style, and meter, and period. We decided to keep only the dream, only the wondering through limbo. What we discovered there was a journey of hapless pain, and some small measure of salvation. Free-versed, the book is entirely different in its form, but – we believe – very close to the experience it describes. It wanted to lose itself, we chose to follow it.

This is why some explanation is in order. First of all, some of it won't make sense. Some of it, for entirely different reasons, did not make sense in Portuguese to begin with. If in English it seems loosely bound up inside the rules of syntax, then in Portuguese it suffers from the opposite curse, and tightly wrapped, almost disappears from any proper context. Do not fret: the words are all there, and if one would like to understand them, one can. But differently from the original, this version bleeds, one line into the next, and – hopefully – wherever you want to meet it, it will meet you there.

The grammatical marks are still kept: exclamations, question marks, commas, semi colons and even the infamously mysterious "…?" are all of them without exception present. They serve now less to convey meanings of excitement or doubt, and more as just that: marks. Landmarks. Traces I leave in a chaotic topographical plane as safe-houses, lighthouses to mark breaths, and help navigate this dream. For this reason, we give you the translation along side the original. They are meant to be read side by side, and if we dare, we should even say they compliment each other: the translation lacks all the beautiful perfectionist structure of the original, reaching for some silver city, emulating the unifying support that binds and brings to becoming all things in existence. However, this translation, we believe, contains something of what the original meant to convey but – in its time – could not: something of the experience of forgetting, as how one would remember reality when trapped in a dream. A dream itself is the world to dreamers, and to attempt a connection to the truth of dreaming is to risk the muddy feeling of wading through limbo: the heavy, awkward experience of being faced with the parts of oneself one cannot conquer; those proprietary logics that belong to history, and to language, much more than to us.

Each author's lexicon was kept consistent, of course, and we attempted translations of all idioms and expressions, but the impersonal subject, and as it presents itself in Portuguese (implied in different parts of the sentence) makes for confusing, broken sentences. Absolutely opposite to the original, even with the same words, even at times, in the same places. One line says: "Where it is suffered, the angst of distance/ From those we love with soul and fervor" (106). The logic of dreaming is built around language, but it does not obey syntactical rules. Dreaming requires the abandonment of syntax for the sake of pursuing the logic of signifiers, of lacking, of emptiness and desire. And if one were so inclined to make that point, one might say that so does living. And so does dying, for that matter.

In that limbo we find the most beautiful moments. Prayers, really. Things one would wish upon their most beloved, and those words, as three dimensional weighty things, have power: "Hymns of love, that the birds might raise you/ From your hymns of placid balance" (100). Ultimately we found the text to be precious because of all the ways it doesn't work. And in that, we found the obvious, simple, material and elegant link between poetry and death: they are both letting go. They are both becoming.

If this is no ordinary book of poetry, it is, of course, because there is no (good) ordinary book of poetry, we must remember. But also for other reasons. If a book can be many things, that this one fits the bill entirely. It's a Discursive Event, it's a Bible. It's a respite, an embarrassment, a leap in the dark. A source of conflict and polemics, a mean addiction. A small measure of hope; a fib. One cannot break away from it all, for still there is a voice in this book, reaching from someplace we cannot fathom to teach us about the absurd in poetry. How even the very most infantile verse can miss the mark and shine. Words are like that, it seems: they will surprise you.

It is important to talk about authors, and in his afterword Jeremy will lead us through that particular limbo much better than I ever could. Except to say this: there are no sentences to translate. Simply put: once looked at closely, texts reveal no sentences. There are only authors. It is them whom we converse with, whom we listen to and argue with. They are the ones who offend us, leave us bleeding without the means to call for help, they are our salvation. Sentences evaporate as soon as you focus on them. They are patterns of possibility of a single unifying position, they are wanting, desire; and we can only translate just that: wanting, desire. We seek it out, it seems: much more than the overestimated desire to cheat death, a most fundamental drive to mean. To mean something. Far over and beyond the problems of structure, phrasing, lexicon, or even interpretation, we have to remember what Lacan kept insisting throughout all his seminars we'd understand: that desire is emptiness, surrounded by words. That was all that was passed on to me through Chico, and so all I can offer to pass on to you.

I would expect to be able to speak for our publisher Vincent, and our writer, Jeremy; when saying I sincerely hope that it suffices; but alas I am reminded of another creature from the Dream World who, of course, already said it best:

If we shadows have offended
Think but this, and all is mended
That you have but slumber'd here
While these visions did appear
And this weak and idle theme

No more yielding but a dream
Gentles, do not reprehend:
if you pardon, we will mend:
...

Oh, well. You know the rest.

– Vitor, Campinas, 18th of August 2013

poetry from beyond the grave

*1742/4 Ignácio José de Alvarenga Peixoto
Revived

Heavenly lyre,
Muse who inspires
My heart
To remember…
Celebrate, serene,
The full life,
The sublime peace,
The light without equal.

Return, again
To the great people
For I do not tire
Of trembling;
Reveal, still,
The beautiful Fatherland
That vibrates
All of my being.

Praise now
The new dawn
That shines full
Of Christian love.
The world at peril

Ignácio José de Alvarenga Peixoto † 1793
Redivivo

Divina lira,
Musa que inspira
Meu coração
A relembrar...
Celebra, amena,
A vida plena,
A paz sublime,
A luz sem par.

Volta, de novo
Ao grande povo
Que não me canso
De estremecer;
Revela, ainda,
A Pátria linda
Que faz vibrar
Todo o meu ser.

Exalça agora
A nova aurora
Que brilha cheia
De amor cristão.
O mundo em prova

Renewing itself
And awaiting the day
Of redemption.

Bind yourself to the chant
Pleasing and holy
That flows proudly,
Beyond the tomb…
Divine lire,
Praise the gospel
Of freedom
In the eternal good.

Speak of the greatness
Of the ignited glory
Of the higher life
That pain produces,
Proclaim to the Earth
That beyond the war
And beyond the night
Blossoms the light.

Do no further seek,
Crying elsewhere,
To weaken yourself,
In the thousand struggles.

Just sing,
Merry and faithful,

Que se renova
Espera o dia
De redenção.

Une-te ao canto
Formoso e santo
Que flui soberbo,
Sepulcro além...
Lira divina,
Louva a doutrina
Da liberdade
No eterno bem.

Dize a grandeza
Da glória acesa
Na vida excelsa
Que a dor produz,
Proclama à Terra
Que além da guerra
E além da noite
Floresce a luz.

Não mais procures,
Chorando alhures,
Enfraquecer-te
Nas lutas mil.

Canta somente,
Ditosa e crente,

The new age
Of my Brazil.

A nova era
Do meu Brasil.

*1762 Souza Caldas
Act of Contrition

To you
Lord,
My God
Of Love
My soul
Begs
Salvation!

My Father,
I know well
That I hardly
Walk,
In search
Of mistakes
And imperfection;

And so
I sinned,
In dark
Erred,
And fair,
Made
Penitence be.

Souza Caldas † 1814
Ato de contrição

A vós
Senhor,
Meu Deus
De Amor,
Minhalma
Implora
A salvação!

Meu Pai,
Bem sei
Que mal
Andei,
Buscando
O erro
E a imperfeição;

Assim
Pequei,
Na treva
Errei,
E jus
Eu fiz
A expiação.

You are,
However,
The beam
Of Good!
I heard
From Heaven
My prayer.

You are
The light,
And by
The cross
Of my
Woe,
I seek forgiveness;

Forgiveness
Which brings
Repose
And peace
To my
Living
In trial.

I beg it
From you,
In the pain
Too deep,
Bitter,

Vós sois,
Porém,
Farol
Do Bem!
Ouvi
Dos Céus
Minha oração.

Sois vós
A luz,
E junto
A cruz
Do meu
Sofrer,
Quero o perdão;

Perdão
Que traz
Sossego
E paz
Ao meu
Viver
Na provação.

Suplico-o
A vós,
Na dor
Atroz,
Amara

And rough
Of contrition!

Give to
My being,
Stricken,
While seeing
Your
Sin,
Redemption;

And I will
Be able
Happily
To defeat
Evil
The cruel
And vicious dragon!

E rude
Da contrição!

Dai ao
Meu ser,
Aflito
Ao ver
O seu
Pecado,
A redenção;

E hei de
Poder
Feliz
Vencer
Do mal
Cruel
O atroz dragão!

* 1807 Álvaro Teixeira de Macedo
After the Party

Do not deliver yourself, on this Earth, to vile lies,
Unburden yourself of the cobweb of human vanity,
For death will soon shame, and disabuse
The madness living in the flesh that raves…

Joy wanes wrath itself,
All vanity throws itself into the abyss,
The flame flickers under a dishonest distortion
Of the truth, heavenly, sovereign.

After the party of terrible, empty laughter,
The soul overflows its grave in tears,
Like a single leaf to a vicious storm.

And those that from light did not build their temples and dens,
Come down, with souls consumed,
In the turmoil of ash and forgetting.

Álvaro Teixeira de Macedo † 1849
Depois da festa

Não te entregues na Terra à vil mentira,
Desfaze a teia da filáucia humana,
Que a Morte, em breve, humilha e desengana
A demência da carne que delira...

O gozo desfalece à própria gana,
Toda vaidade ao báratro se atira,
Sob a ilusão mendaz chameja a pira
Da verdade, celeste, soberana.

Finda a festa de baldo riso infando,
A alma transpõe o túmulo chorando,
Qual folha solta ao furacão violento.

E quem da luz não fez templo e guarida,
Desce gemendo, de alma consumida,
Ao turbilhão de cinza e esquecimento.

* 1839 Casimiro de Abreu
To My Land

What tender golden dream
From my lovely hours,
In the shelter of the palm trees
Of my beloved Brazil!
Life was a beautiful day
In a garden of flowers,
Filled with scent and wonder
Under spring skies.

Childhood, a cool lake
Where existence begins,
Where the swans of innocence
Drink the nectar of love.
Boyhood, a hymn
Of soft melodies,
Made of bird songs
And the perfume of flowers.

The day, a smiling morning,
In a song of dawn;
The starry night
After the sweet sunset;
And in the dear landscape,

Casimiro de Abreu † 1860
À minha terra

Que terno sonho dourado
Das minhas horas fagueiras,
No recanto das palmeiras
Do meu querido Brasil!
A vida era um dia lindo
Num vergel cheio de flores,
Cheio de aroma e esplendores
Sob um céu primaveril.

A infância, um lago tranqüilo
Onde começa a existência,
Onde os cisnes da inocência
Bebem o néctar do amor.
A mocidade era um hino
De melodias suaves,
Formadas de trinos de aves
E de perfumes de flor.

O dia, manhã ridente,
Numa canção de alvorada;
A noite toda estrelada
Após o doce arrebol;
E na paisagem querida,

The branches of orange groves
And the thick mango trees
Shine golden under the sun!

Oh! What a blaze in the soul,
Constantly pondering,
Thoughts dreaming
And the heart put to song,
In the delicate harmony
That was born out of the beauty,
Of Nature's green,
And the beautiful ocean's green!

Oh! What poem the being
Of childhood and boyhood,
Of tenderness and longing,
Of sadness and joy;
Like a wondrous chanting,
With the chorus inspired
By evening and night,
The dusk and the dawn.

I remember it all and so sharply!
The clarity of lakes,
The fondling, caresses
And my mother's kisses!
The singing from hooded siskins,
The melody of the springs,

Os ramos das laranjeiras
E das frondosas mangueiras
Douradas à luz do Sol!

Oh! que clarão dentro d'alma,
Constantemente cismando,
O pensamento sonhando
E o coração a cantar,
Na delicada harmonia
Que nascia da beleza,
Do verde da Natureza,
Do verde do lindo mar!

Oh! que poema a existência
De infância e de mocidade,
De ternura e de saudade,
De tristeza e de prazer;
Igual a um canto sublime,
Como uma estrofe inspirada
Na noite e na madrugada,
Na tarde e no amanhecer.

De tudo me lembro e quanto!
A transparência dos lagos,
As carícias, os afagos
E os beijos de minha mãe!
Dos trinos dos pintassilgos,
Da melodia das fontes,

The clouds near the horizon
Lost in the blue beyond.

When I crossed the meadows,
Without the shadows of pain,
Barefoot, my chest to the wind,
In a sweet and happy day!
The blossoming peach trees,
The tops brimming with mulberries,
The cloak of light from dawn,
The squawking quail-doves!

If death routs the body,
It does not rout remembrance:
Hope never ends,
Dreaming never ends!
And to my dearest land,
Speckled in palm trees,
I hope, in my loveliest hours,
To one day, return.

As nuvens nos horizontes
Perdidos no azul do além.

Quando eu cruzava as campinas,
Sem sombras de sofrimento,
Descalço, com o peito ao vento,
Num tempo doce e feliz!
Os pessegueiros floridos,
As frondes cheias de amora,
O manto de luz da aurora,
Os pios das juritis!

Se a morte aniquila o corpo,
Não aniquila a lembrança:
Jamais se extingue a esperança,
Nunca se extingue o sonhar!
E à minha terra querida,
Recortada de palmeiras,
Espero em horas fagueiras
Um dia poder voltar.

* 1847 Castro Alves
Let Us March!

There are wondering mysteries
In the mysteries of destinies
That send us to rebirth:
From the Maker's light we're born,
Multiple lives we lead,
To return to that same light.

We search in Mankind
The truths of the Truth,
Thirsty for love and peace;
And amidst the living-dead
We are suffering captives
Of unfairness and pain.

It is the everlasting, holy struggle,
In which the Spirit stirs
In the web of evolution;
The workshop where the incarcerated soul
Forges the light, and forges the greatness
Of sublime perfection.

It is the drop of water falling
In the rising shrub,

Castro Alves †1871
Marchemos!

Há mistérios peregrinos
No mistério dos destinos
Que nos mandam renascer:
Da luz do Criador nascemos,
Múltiplas vidas vivemos,
Para à mesma luz volver.

Buscamos na Humanidade
As verdades da Verdade,
Sedentos de paz e amor;
E em meio dos mortos-vivos
Somos míseros cativos
Da iniqüidade e da dor.

É a luta eterna e bendita,
Em que o Espírito se agita
Na trama da evolução;
Oficina onde a alma presa
Forja a luz, forja a grandeza
Da sublime perfeição.

É a gota d'água caindo
No arbusto que vai subindo,

Full of sap and saplings;
The bit of manure,
That turns to perfume
On the flower's crown.

The flower that, expiring tender,
Falls to the soil impregnating
The tough ground that produces,
And leaving the softest scent
In the fleeting breeze,
Of the lit nights.

It is the unbending anvil, and hammer,
By the toils of labor,
The bread-making grubber;
The chisel of sculptors
Turning stone to flowers,
In Droves of choices.

It is the pain that through the years,
Of executioners and tyrants,
Sweet angels make,
Changing the dimmest Neros,
To virtues' heralds,
And messengers of peace.

Everything evolves, and everything dreams
In the funny, constant yearning
To reach higher, achieve more;

Pleno de seiva e verdor;
O fragmento do estrume,
Que se transforma em perfume
Na corola de uma flor.

A flor que, terna, expirando,
Cai ao solo fecundando
O chão duro que produz,
Deixando um aroma leve
Na aragem que passa breve,
Nas madrugadas de luz.

É a rija bigorna, o malho,
Pelas fainas do trabalho,
A enxada fazendo o pão;
O escopro dos escultores
Transformando a pedra em flores,
Em Carraras de eleição.

É a dor que através dos anos,
Dos algozes, dos tiranos,
Anjos puríssimos faz,
Transmutando os Neros rudes
Em arautos de virtudes,
Em mensageiros de paz.

Tudo evolui, tudo sonha
Na imortal ânsia risonha
De mais subir, mais galgar;

Life is light and wonder,
God is the love in it.
And the Universe, its altar.

And on Earth, sometimes are lit
Bright beacons that burst,
Inside the mortal dark;
Their flaming passage
Leave flashes and pictures,
In eternal echoes.

It's the suffering of the Christ,
Wonderful and never seen,
In the sacrifice of the cross,
The definition of piety,
Whose love for the Truth
No punishment captures.

It is Socrates and the hemlock.
It is Caesar and his warring,
Warrior and tyrant;
It is Cellini and his art,
Or the sword of Bonaparte,
The great conqueror.

It is the clergy taking over,
And in catechism teaching
The hapless savage;
It is the lesson of humility,

A vida é luz, esplendor,
Deus somente é o seu amor,
O Universo é o seu altar.

Na Terra, às vezes se acendem
Radiosos faróis que esplendem
Dentro das trevas mortais;
Suas rútilas passagens
Deixam fulgores, imagens,
Em reflexos perenais.

É o sofrimento do Cristo,
Portentoso, jamais visto,
No sacrifício da cruz,
Sintetizando a piedade,
E cujo amor à Verdade
Nenhuma pena traduz.

É Sócrates e a cicuta,
É César trazendo a luta,
Tirânico e lutador;
É Cellini com sua arte,
Ou o sabre de Bonaparte,
O grande conquistador.

É Anchieta dominando,
A ensinar catequizando
O selvagem infeliz;
É a lição da humildade,

And extreme charity
Of the poor man of Assisi.

Oh! Blessed he who teaches,
Who struggles, who shines,
Who sows the light and goodness.
Through the toils of evolving:
He will have the venture he yearns for
On the pathways of moving on.

A soaring voice sounds,
Across the Universe it echoes:
– "Forward, march on!
Love is the light one reaches,
Keeping faith, and keeping hope,
Towards the Infinite, march on!"

De extremosa caridade
Do pobrezinho de Assis.

Oh! bendito quem ensina,
Quem luta, quem ilumina,
Quem o bem e a luz semeia
Nas fainas do evolutir:
Terá a ventura que anseia.
Nas sendas do progredir.

Uma excelsa voz ressoa,
No Universo inteiro ecoa:
– "Para a frente caminhai!
O amor é a luz que se alcança,
Tende fé, tende esperança,
Para o Infinito marchai!"

*1839   Júlio Diniz
Birds and Angels

Birdies… Birdies…
Nuzzled in their nests,
Homes of love, sweet and lax,
Tiny little bards
Between trees and flowers,
Singing…
Singing…

Children, soft angels,
As tender as flocks of birds
Through a clear and beautiful sky,
Scented amaryllis,
Petals full of dew,
Smiling…
Smiling…

Tender hymn of hope
From birds and children,
Blends itself with the light
Weaving the hourse serene,
Of earthly joys,
Smiling…
Singing…

Júlio Diniz † 1871
Aves e anjos

Passarinhos… passarinhos…
Aconchegados nos ninhos,
Lares de amor doce e brando,
Pequeninos trovadores
Entre as árvores e as flores,
Cantando…
Cantando…

Crianças, anjos suaves,
Mimosas quais bandos de aves
Cortando um céu claro e lindo,
Açucenas perfumadas,
Com as pétalas orvalhadas,
Sorrindo….
Sorrindo…

Hino terno de esperanças
Das aves e das crianças,
Vai-se com a luz misturando,
Tecendo as horas serenas
Das alegrias terrenas,
Sorrindo…
Cantando…

* 1841   Fagundes Varela
          Immortality

Lord! Lord! May the shining verbs
Of love, perfection, and freedom,
Inflame my voices in this instant!
That my yelp, aloud, may rise,
Leading the helping message
Of hope to Mankind!
Lord! Lord! May it hover over the world,
The light of your unequaled power,
That the lilacs may salute you spreading their scent
Over sunrises, nights, and dawns;

Hymns of love, that the birds my raise you
From your hymns of placid balance;
That the springs, in their sweet murmur
Bless you with tender softness;
And that all beings of this world find themselves
Before your transcendent majesty
Saturated by the all-powerful love
Proceeding, plentiful, from thy breast!...

Lord! May my loud voice
Spread among men; and may the truth
Shine in the land of bitter!

Fagundes Varela † 1875
Imortalidade

Senhor! Senhor! que os verbos luminosos
Do amor, da perfeição, da liberdade,
Inflamem minhas vozes neste instante!
Que o meu grito bem alto se levante,
Conduzindo a mensagem benfazeja
Das esperanças para a Humanidade!
Senhor! Senhor! que paire sobre o mundo
A luz do teu poder inigualável,
Que os lírios te saúdem perfumando
Os arrebóis, as noites, as auroras;

Hinos de amor, que os pássaros te elevem
Dos seus ninhos de plácida harmonia;
Que as fontes no seu doce murmúrio
Te bendigam com terna suavidade;
Que todo o ser no mundo se descubra
Perante a tua excelsa majestade,
Saturado do amor onipotente
Que promana abundante do teu seio!...

Senhor! que a minha voz altissonante
Se propague entre os homens; que a verdade
Resplandeça na terra da amargura!

Oh, Father! You, who undoes the impossible,
And turns into roses, thorns,
And that beats away the dark from our paths
With the light that proves your omnipotence.
Allow my soul to be heard
In the vastness of the world of banishment;
So that my brothers on Earth may welcome me
As the invisible absent, alive again!...

Brethren, here I am again at your side!
I come from lucid, splendid spheres,
I have crossed gloomy roads
And starry, wondrous fissures,
Wielding the psalms of hope.

I could overcome abysses of gold and roses,
Fissures of dream and dark chasms,
Planets like vessels without pilots
On the oceans of Endless ether.
I have gazed the haunting Milky Ways,
Visions of eternal suns confused
Among fiery, distant stars;
I have seen prodigious stars firing
Harmonies of love and clarity,
And humanities among humanities
Populating the splendorous Universe...

I have rested on islands of repose,
In beautiful distant archipelagos,

Ó Pai! tu que removes o impossível,
Que transmudas em rosas os espinhos,
E que espancas a treva dos caminhos
Com a luz que afirma a tua onipotência,
Permite que minhalma seja ouvida
Na vastidão do mundo do desterro;
Que os meus irmãos da Terra me recebam
Como o ausente invisível, redivivo!...

Irmãos, eis-me de novo ao vosso lado!
Venho de esferas lúcidas, radiosas,
Atravessei estradas tenebrosas
E sendas deslumbrantes e estelíferas,
Empunhando o saltério da esperança.

Pude transpor abismos de ouro e rosas,
Sendas de sonho e báratros escuros,
Planetas como naus sem palinuros
Nos oceanos do éter Infinito!
Contemplei Vias-Lácteas assombrosas,
Visões de sóis eternos, confundidas
Entre estrelas igníferas, distantes;
Vastros portentosos, desferindo
Harmonias de amor e claridades,
E humanidades entre humanidades
Povoando o Universo esplendoroso...

Descansei sobre as ilhas de repouso,
Em lindos arquipélagos distantes,

Inhabited, enchanted palaces,
In retreats of calm and peaceful love,
Where the soil is gold and snow,
Where the darkness and the night are only
Memories of obscure worlds!
Where the flowers of undying affection
Do not wither as on Earth.
There, on these lucid, holy orbs,
Love, and only love, nurtures and gives life.

Only love is the vibration of everything!
I have seen skies over skies, innumerable,
Worlds of pain, and worlds of joy,
In bright lights and harmonies
And the archangelic kisses of light,
Which are the messages of God spread everywhere!
And I have only seen a fraction,
A minuscule detail, a fragment
Of the endless shining Creation!

Ah! Death!... Death is the bright angel
Of honest, joyful freedom,
When we wait for it sad and weary;
When it brings us spotless and sublime
The flame of hope inside the soul,
And in loving in life its most noble goods,
And if the world stifles in us all joy,
Stealing from us consolations and affections,

Habitei os palácios encantados,
Em retiros de amor calmo e sereno,
Onde o solo é formado de ouro e neve,
Onde a treva e onde a noite são apenas
Recordações de mundos obscuros!
Onde as flores do afeto imperecível
Não se emurchecem como sobre a Terra.
Lá, nesses orbes lúcidos, divinos,
O amor, somente o amor, nutre e dá vida.

Somente o amor é a vibração de tudo!
Vi céus por sobre céus inumeráveis,
Mundos de dor e mundos de alegria,
Em luminosidades e harmonias
Aos beijos arcangélicos da luz,
Que é mensagem de Deus por toda a parte!
E apenas conheci um pormenor,
Um detalhe minúsculo, um fragmento
Da Criação infinita e resplendente.

Ah! Morte!... A Morte é o anjo luminoso
Da liberdade franca, jubilosa,
Quando a esperamos tristes e abatidos;
Quando nos traz imácula e sublime
A chama da esperança dentro d'alma,
Amando-se da vida os bens mais nobres,
Se o mundo abafa em nós toda a alegria,
Roubando-nos afetos e consolos,

Martyrizing the pained heart
On the cross of most austere sufferings.

Death corroborates our faith,
Our deepest hopes,
Braking the veil that covers from our sight
The eternal landscape of the Universe,
And death points to us the sky, the immensity,
Where the happy soul grows grander,
Leading other souls in mazes
To the light, to life and love!

What is Earth, before the grandeur
Of so many suns and orbs of light?
It is only a small instance
Where the pain and where the tear divine
Shape the soul towards perfection;

It is only one step in the immensity,
Where one may regenerate, in torment
If one is away from the Light and the truth;
It is only a transitory exile,
Where it is suffered, the angst of distance
From those we love with full soul and fervor.

Death! May it bless you, sufferers,
And may the weary spirit bless you,
Since you are the freeing hand
From the slaves of flesh, the slaves

Martirizando o coração dorido
Na cruz dos sofrimentos mais austeros.

A morte corrobora as nossas crenças,
As nossas esperanças mais profundas,
Rompendo o véu que encobre à nossa vista
O eterno panorama do Universo,
E aponta-nos o céu, a imensidade,
Onde as almas ditosas se engrandecem,
Outras almas guiando em labirintos
Para a luz, para a vida e para o amor!

Que representa a Terra, ante a grandeza
De tantos sóis e orbes luminosos?
É somente uma estância pequenina
Onde a dor e onde a lágrima divina
Modelam almas para a perfeição;

É apenas um degrau na imensidade,
Onde se regenera no tormento
Quem se afasta da Luz e da verdade;
Ela é somente o exílio temporário,
Onde se sofre a angústia da distância
Dos que amamos com alma e com fervor.

Morte! que te abençoem sofredores,
Que te bendiga o espírito abatido,
Já que és a terna mão libertadora
Dos escravos da carne, dos escravos

Of afflictions, pains, and torture!
I bless you for all that you have given me:
For the beauty of immortality,
For the vision of splendorous skies,
For the kisses of the beloved beings.

Lord! Lord! May my voice extend,
Like a sublime song of hope,
Over the brows of all who suffer,
Yearning for more light, more freedom
In the orb of expiation and mercilessness!

Das aflições, das dores, da tortura!
Bendigo-te por tudo o que me deste:
Pela beleza da imortalidade,
Pela visão dos céus resplandecentes,
Pelos beijos dos seres bem-amados.

Senhor! Senhor! que a minha voz se estenda,
Como um canto sublime de esperança,
Sobre a fronte de todos quantos sofrem,
Ansiando mais luz, mais liberdade
No orbe da expiação e da impiedade!

*1842 Antero de Quental
       To Death

Oh Death, I have loved you as if you were
The end of the dark winding road,
Where lives the endless peace of Nothing
Away from unsatisfied distress.

It was you, the worshipped sight
That smiled in the pain of my hours,
Vision of sad brooding faces,
In the sheets of bound-up Silence.

I sought you, I who carried a dead soul,
Beaten in suffering,
Beating, ramped, at your door;

And you opened the dark, cold door wide,
From which I entered into Suffering,
In a hollow; sadder and darker.

Antero de Quental † 1891
À morte

Ó Morte, eu te adorei, como se foras
O Fim da sinuosa e negra estrada,
Onde habitasse a eterna paz do Nada
As agonias desconsoladoras.

Eras tu a visão idolatrada
Que sorria na dor das minhas horas,
Visão de tristes faces cismadoras,
Nos crepes do Silêncio amortalhada.

Busquei-te, eu que trazia a alma já morta,
Escorraçada no padecimento,
Batendo alucinado à tua porta;

E escancaraste a porta escura e fria,
Por onde penetrei no Sofrimento,
Numa senda mais triste e mais sombria.

*1834   Bittencourt Sampaio
To Mary

Here it is, my Lady, the poor caravan
Gathered in earnest supplication,
Begging for the piety, the peace, and the life
Of your sovereign charity.

Strengthen our aching souls
In the redemption of human injustice,
With the balm of belief that emanates
From the light of the enlightened kindness.

Providence of all the tortured,
I heard from the Heavens, happy and endless,
Our honest prayers to the Lord…

That our caravan of Truth
Aid the Good of Mankind,
In this mystic feast of love.

Bittencourt Sampaio † 1895
A Maria

Eis-nos, Senhora, a pobre caravana
Em fervorosas súplicas, reunida,
Implorando a piedade, a paz e a vida,
De vossa caridade soberana.

Fortalecei-nos a alma dolorida
Na redenção da iniqüidade humana,
Com o bálsamo da crença que promana
Das luzes da bondade esclarecida.

Providência de todos os aflitos,
Ouvi dos Céus, ditosos e infinitos,
Nossas sinceras preces ao Senhor...

Que a nossa caravana da Verdade
Colabore no Bem da Humanidade,
Neste banquete místico do amor.

* 1830 João de Deus
Poetry from Beyond the Grave

Beyond the grave, the Spirit still sings
Its ideals of peace, of love and light,
In the happy country where Jesus
Rules with sacrosanct kindness.

In these mansions, the lyre rises
Glorifying the love in which God shines,
To sing out the Good that leads us
To divine joy, pure and holy.

From this eternal Spring of Harmony
Overflows the sublime light of Poetry,
And floods the Earth with splendor.

Sparse hymns of hope
About men, bringing them closer,
In their ascent towards Beauty and Love.

João de Deus † 1896
Parnaso de Além-Túmulo

Além do túmulo o Espírito inda canta
Seus ideais de paz, de amor e luz,
No ditoso país onde Jesus
Impera com bondade sacrossanta.

Nessas mansões, a lira se levanta
Glorificando o Amor que em Deus transluz,
Para o Bem exalçar, que nos conduz
À divina alegria, pura e santa.

Dessa Castélia eterna da Harmonia
Transborda a luz excelsa da Poesia,
Que a Terra toda inunda de esplendor.

Hinos das esperanças espargidos
Sobre os homens, tornando-os mais unidos,
Na ascensão para o Belo e para o Amor.

* 1847   Lucindo Filho
          No Shadows

Next to the grave where longing cries
And where the dream of tears ends,
It opens, the door to the godly mansion
Carved out of reflections of dawn.

No longer night; it lives in everything, now,
But the deep and wondering beauty,
Wrapped around the emerald light
Of shuddering, splendorous hope.

Without the shadows of inhuman struggles,
The victorious soul chants hymns,
Drunk with peace and immortality.

Do not mourn those leaving at day's end,
That the cold grave in dark grey
Is the new door to eternity.

Lucindo Filho † 1896
Sem sombras

Junto ao sepulcro onde a saudade chora
E onde o sonho das lágrimas termina,
Abre-se a porta da mansão divina
Entalhada em reflexos de aurora.

Não mais a noite; vive em tudo, agora,
A beleza profunda e peregrina,
Envolvida na luz esmeraldina
Da esperança que vibra e resplendora.

Sem as sombras das lutas desumanas,
A alma vitoriosa entoa hosanas,
Ébria de paz e de imortalidade.

Não lamenteis quem parta ao fim do dia,
Que a sepultura em cinza escura e fria
É a nova porta para a eternidade.

* 1845 Luiz Guimarães Junior
Sonnet

In the dark of the tempestuous years,
Of the old age of the ill-lived days,
I have wanted to return to times now gone
Of youth, to plentiful times.

Little could I gage that other joys, still,
Far more sublime than those already savored
In the stretch of forgotten weeping,
I would find in the wonderful heavens.

To hover in the Beyond!… return to the first home,
Reemerged in eternal youth,
A flash of peace for a poor wanderer!

And upon the edge of the amplitudes of the Heights
I pierced, gleaming the Immensity,
Sobbing, eager of happiness.

Luiz Guimarães Junior † 1898
Soneto

Na escuridão dos anos procelosos,
Da velhice nos dias mal vividos,
Eu quisera voltar aos tempos idos
Da juventude, aos tempos bonançosos.

Mal podia julgar que inda outros gozos
Mais sublimes que aqueles já fruídos,
Nas esteiras de prantos esquecidos,
Acharia nos céus maravilhosos.

Pairar no Além!... volver ao lar primeiro,
Ressurgido em perene mocidade,
Clarão de paz ao pobre caminheiro!

No limiar das amplidões da Altura
Penetrei, vislumbrando a Imensidade,
Soluçando empolgado de ventura.

* 1861 Cruz e Souza
Heaven

There is a heaven for the Spirit who struggles
In the ocean of saving tears,
A heaven filled with bright lights and life,
That crowns the spotless soul with light.

The song of triumph is heard there,
The song of souls free from pains and punishments,
Souls that make life the web of splendors,
In almost full and perfect peace.

Think, oh weary walkers,
That on Earth, you live as foreigners,
Of tired souls and aching hearts:

Think, while you look at the endless height,
The wondrous orbs of ventures
Suspended, between suns, in the Infinite!

Cruz e Souza † 1898
Céu

Há um céu para o Espírito que luta
No oceano dos prantos salvadores,
Céu repleto de vida e de fulgores,
Que coroa de luz a alma impoluta.

A canção da vitória ali se escuta,
Da alma livre das penas e das dores,
Que faz da vida a rede de esplendores,
Na paz quase integral e absoluta.

Considerai, ó pobres caminheiros,
Que na Terra viveis como estrangeiros,
De alma ofegante e coração aflito:

Considerai, fitando a imensa altura,
Os deslumbrantes orbes da ventura
Por entre os sóis suspensos no Infinito!

*1875   José Duro
        To Men

Back to dust, man that comes in rush,
To seek the key to the riddle that hides
The arrest of death, the beyond the Earth,
Where the dream ends, and life begins anew.

Back to the cruel slumber of your dark flesh,
Break with your weeping the daily bread,
Begone with your sickness on the dark road,
To later hear the voice of the grave.

Resign, lay your hands on your own wounds,
Roam in the pain of your cursed night,
Because the darkness and the suffering will always follow you!

Acknowledge how ignorant you are, still.
Life is unlimited and endless tremor,
And its great mystery is everywhere…

José Duro † 1899
Aos homens

Volta ao pó dos mortais, homem que vens, depressa,
A chave procurar do enigma que encerra
A paragem da morte, o mais além da Terra,
Onde o sonho termina e a vida recomeça.

Volve ao sono cruel da tua carne obscura,
Amassa com o teu pranto o pão de cada dia,
Vai com o teu padecer sobre a estrada sombria,
Para depois ouvir a voz da sepultura.

Tomé, coloca as mãos na tua própria chaga,
Perambula na dor da tua noite aziaga,
Porque a treva e o sofrer sempre hão de acompanhar-te!

Reconhece o quanto és ignorante ainda.
A vida é vibração ilimitada, infinda,
E o seu grande mistério existe em toda parte…

* 1867 Antônio Nobre
Sonnet

"When the ground is covered in dead leaves
My heart said in grave tone –
Extinguishing the life that comprises you,
You shall sleep in my bosom the last sleep…"

And murmured the soul – "Ended the Fall,
Spring comes through other doors;
In the grave, there is no abandonment,
Or the rough and bitter pain with which you punish yourself."

I heard these voices, moved,
Dying of angst, dying of doubt,
Waiting out the sunset, sadden;

And beyond the bitter life of seconds,
I arose from the torture and the sadness,
Under the healthy airs of other worlds!

Antônio Nobre † 1900
Soneto

"Quando cobrir-se o chão de folhas mortas –
Meu coração dizia em grave entono –
Extinguindo-se a vida que comportas,
Dormirás no meu seio o último sono…

E murmurava a alma – "Findo o Outono,
A Primavera vem por outras portas;
Não existe no túmulo o abandono,
Ou a dor amarga e rude em que te cortas."

Escutava essas vozes comovido,
Morto de angústia, morto de incerteza,
Aguardando o sol-posto, entristecido;

E além da amarga vida de segundos,
Ressurgi da tortura e da tristeza,
Sob os ares sadios de outros mundos!

*1876   Auta de Souza
        Godspeed

The bell rings in sweet softness,
In the healing place of a church;
In between its wings, at the altar, soars
The scent of the pleasures of longing for.

Moans the widow, pines the orphan;
And the soul that returned from exile kisses
The light that gleams and grows stronger,
In the blue cathedral of immensity.

"Godspeed, Earth of my misadventures…
Godspeed, my beloved…" – says from the heights
The freed soul, the sailing blue sky…

– "Godspeed…" – cry the leafless roses,
– "Godspeed…" – yelp the hopeless voices
Of those still left in exile, delaying…

Auta de Souza † 1901
Adeus

O sino plange em terna suavidade,
No ambiente balsâmico da igreja;
Entre as naves, no altar, em tudo adeja
O perfume dos goivos da saudade.

Geme a viuvez, lamenta-se a orfandade;
E a alma que regressou do exílio beija
A luz que resplandece, que viceja,
Na catedral azul da imensidade.

"Adeus, Terra das minhas desventuras...
Adeus, amados meus..." – diz nas alturas
A alma liberta, o azul do céu singrando...

– "Adeus..." – choram as rosas desfolhadas,
– "Adeus..." – clamam as vozes desoladas
De quem ficou no exílio soluçando...

* 1853　José do Patrocínio
　　　　　New Abolition

The merciless, raw slavery proceeds…
No longer an inhuman, dark and hostile slave house.
The miscomprehension of love, however, continues
In the cruel realm of which the darkness is proud.

But the light of the Lord does not fear, or retreat,
In angst and pain, sublime, it adorns itself,
And, from the graces of temples to the mockery of streets,
Freedom rises, august and sovereign…

Brothers of my Brazil, enchanted and divine,
From Amazonas to the Prata rises towards God, a hymn
That brings out the greatness of a people in the Gospel!

Let us smite evil, and fight disbelief,
Unveiling, beyond the closing night,
The happy dawn of a new, free world.

José do Patrocínio † 1905
Nova Abolição

Prossegue a escravidão implacável e crua...
Não mais senzala hostil, escura e desumana.
A incompreensão do amor, no entanto, continua
Em domínio cruel de que a treva se ufana.

Mas a luz do Senhor não teme, nem recua,
Na ansiedade e na dor, sublime, se engalana,
E, das graças do templo aos sarcasmos da rua,
Erige a liberdade augusta e soberana...

Irmãos do meu Brasil, encantado e divino,
Do Amazonas ao Prata ergue-se a Deus um hino
Que exalça no Evangelho a grandeza de um povo!

Fustiguemos o mal, combatendo a descrença,
Descortinando, além da noite que se adensa,
A alvorada feliz de um mundo livre e novo.

*1861 Edmundo Xavier de Barros
Faced with the Earth

Fleeing, though in the light of endless godly gifts,
Without stealing away, though in the struggle that improves,
Man is the sower of his own destiny,
A sad bird in the night, dodging the dawn…

Round the Earth, the stars sing their hymns,
Praising light, where Truth resides,
But in the realm of flesh, beastly drives
Parade a weeping gloom!

It is necessary to conquer on the petrifying junctions,
To sanctify pain, tears and dreams,
To cross the deep and burning chasm of hell,

To witness the extent of the thick and strange night,
That the servants of evil and children of despair
Have, godless, spread across the face of the world!…

Edmundo Xavier de Barros † 1905
Diante da Terra

Fugindo embora à paz de eternos dons divinos,
Sem furtar-se, porém, à luta que aprimora,
O homem é o semeador dos seus próprios destinos,
Ave triste da noite, esquivando-se à aurora...

Em derredor da Terra, estrelas cantam hinos,
Glorificando a luz onde a Verdade mora,
Mas no plano da carne os impulsos tigrinos
Fazem a ostentação da miséria que chora!

Necessário vencer nos vórtices medonhos,
Santificar a dor, as lágrimas e os sonhos,
Do inferno atravessar o abismo ígneo e fundo,

Para ver a extensão da noite estranha e densa,
Que os servos da maldade e os filhos da descrença
Estenderam, sem Deus, sobre a fronte do mundo!...

* 1855 Artur Azevedo
Miniatures of the Elegant Society

I

Adriano Gonçalves de Macedo,
Man of means and no wisdom in the soul,
Entered his room with a smile
At ten in the night, very scared.

A lover's letter – it was a secret –
He would open it, and so it was needed
That his wife, a lady and prudent,
Did not see it, not even as a joke:

Mrs. Corália Augusta Colavida.
Would she be, at this time, in bed?
Lifted the curtain slowly…

But what a tragedy after this danger…
Saw his wife kissing his dear friend
Over the sofa of the dining room.

Artur Azevedo † 1908
Miniaturas da sociedade elegante

I

Adriano Gonçalves de Macedo,
Homem de cabedais e alma sem siso,
Penetrou no seu quarto com um sorriso
Às dez horas da noite, muito a medo.

Uma carta de amante – era um segredo –
Ia abri-la, e, assim, era preciso
Que a sua esposa, dama de juízo,
Não na visse nem mesmo por brinquedo:

Dona Corália Augusta Colavida
Estaria nessa hora recolhida?
Levantou a cortina, devagar...

Mas, que tragédia após esse perigo...
Viu que a esposa beijava um seu amigo,
Sobre o divã, da sala de jantar.

II

In the beautiful mansion of Furtado,
Pranced about the gallant Mariquita
With a queer and common fellow, far too groomed,
A vain and lovesick graduate.

From over the great and pretty dresser,
The young man takes a bound booklet,
And interested, he plays with it,
But the lady, very afflicted, takes it back:

"This book, Antonico, is my dear and private one!"
Says she, nervous. And he, sharp and cheating,
Robs it from her shaky fragile hands:

Opened it. The more he looked the more he laughed…
It was a compendium of pornography,
Filled with indecent portraits.

III

Dom Castilho, renowned Latinist,
Threw a placid conference,
On some rigid moral subject,
Protected by the members of the council.

It was a success. And Ana Fulgência, his wife,
Saw in him a great artist's soul,
Praising in him his most useful being
Of righteous man, and notable writer.

II
No belo palacete do Furtado,
Palestrava a galante Mariquita
Com um pelintra afetado, assaz catita,
Bacharel delambido e enamorado.

De sobre a grande cômoda bonita,
Toma o moço um livrinho encadernado,
Revirando-o nas mãos, interessado,
Mas a jovem retoma-o, muito aflita:

"Esse livro, Antonico, é meu breviário!"
Diz inquieta. E ele, cínico e falsário,
Arrebata-o às frágeis mãos trementes

Abriu-o. Mais o olhava e mais se ria...
Era um compêndio de pornografia,
Recamado de quadros indecentes.

III
Dom Castilho, notável latinista,
Realizara alentada conferência,
Sobre rígido assunto moralista,
Protegido dos membros da regência.

Foi um sucesso. E a esposa Ana Fulgência,
Nele via uma grande alma de artista,
Louvando-lhe a utilíssima existência
De homem probo e notável publicista.

What sharpness of morals! And the colleagues,
Writers, poets, councilmen,
Came to take to him warm embraces.

And in a hurried dash, these gentlemen
Came to find him in his underwear,
In the dark quarters of the maid…

Que primor de moral! e os companheiros
Escritores, poetas, conselheiros,
Foram levar-lhe um abraço camarada.

Numa corrida louca, esses senhores
Foram achá-lo em seus trajes menores,
No apartamento escuro da criada…

* 1844 Cornélio Bastos
Fear Not

Only with Jesus does the tired soul
Return to the shores of love from the sea of life,
And the wondering traveler finds the road,
The leads him back to the shaken land.

Hope, postponed and dried up,
Blossoms again to the blaze of a new dawn;
All the labor and pain of human toil
Make up the light of the desired victory.

Without Jesus, the darkness grows among the wreckage;
Love the cross that weighs upon your shoulders,
Traverse the coarse and merciless desert.

Is the grief still great, each day?
Do not waste the Sweet Company,
Go with Jesus! Fear not! Just believe!

Cornélio Bastos † 1909
Não temas

Somente com Jesus a alma cansada
Volve à praia do amor no mar da vida,
O viajor errante encontra a estrada,
Que o reconduz à terra estremecida.

A esperança, adiada e emurchecida,
Refloresce ao clarão de outra alvorada;
Todo o trabalho e dor da humana lida
São luzes da vitória desejada.

Sem Jesus, cresce a treva entre os escombros;
Ama a cruz que te pesa sobre os ombros,
Vence o deserto áspero e inclemente.

A aflição inda é grande em cada dia?
Não desprezes a Doce Companhia,
Vai com Jesus! não temas! crê somente!

*1859 Raimundo Correia
Sonnets

I

Everything passes in the world. Man passes
Behind the years without understanding them;
Time and pain strike at his hair,
Under the loose light of a rarefied road.

Under misfortune, under the stumbling
Of pain that poisons dream and grace,
It is torn, the fantasy which wraps around him,
And watches as they die, his most beautiful ideals!…

Far from broken illusions, however,
Death shows him more perfect lives,
After the nightmares of cold hands…

And like the feeble little angel that is reborn,
Weeps, weeps and smiles, as if finding
The first light of first days.

Raimundo Correia † 1911
Sonetos

I
Tudo passa no mundo. O homem passa
Atrás dos anos sem compreendê-los;
O tempo e a dor alvejam-lhe os cabelos,
À frouxa luz de uma ventura escassa.

Sob o infortúnio, sob os atropelos
Da dor que lhe envenena o sonho e a graça,
Rasga-se a fantasia que o enlaça,
E vê morrer seus ideais mais belos!...

Longe, porém, das ilusões desfeitas,
Mostra-lhe a morte vidas mais perfeitas,
Depois do pesadelo das mãos frias...

E como o anjinho débil que renasce,
Chora, chora e sorri, qual se encontrasse
A luz primeira dos primeiros dias.

II

Ah!… if the Earth had love, if each
Man thought about other's torment,
If all was love, if each bosom
Of each mother would nourish orphans… If on the road

Of contrast and pain there were the yearning
For the good, that supports the tortured life,
That has never seen a beam of dawn
Inside the endless night which is its portion

From the suffering which no one knows…
Ah! If men would love each other in this instance
The pain would then vanish…

Existence would be burning prayer
Lifted up to God from the bosom of plenty,
Between the hymns of peace and joy.

II
Ah!… se a Terra tivesse o amor, se cada
Homem pensasse no tormento alheio,
Se tudo fosse amor, se cada seio
De mãe nutrisse os órfãos… Se na estrada

Do contraste e da dor houvesse o anseio
Do bem, que ampara a vida torturada,
Que jamais viu um raio de alvorada
Dentro da noite eterna que lhe veio

Do sofrimento que ninguém conhece…
Ah! se os homens se amassem nessa estância
A dor então desapareceria…

A existência seria a ardente prece
Erguida a Deus do seio da abundância,
Entre os hinos da paz e da alegria.

* 1880 Casimiro Cunhia
The Mistake

Sometimes says Science
That belief is a profound mistake,
Waiting for another life
On other planes, in another world…

And says arrogantly to Faith:

– "Thou art mad! Death is only
The endless tranquil sleep
After earthly struggles."

To which it replies, humbly:

– "Later, my friend Science,
You shall be the twin of Faith,
And walk by my side.
If it is sleep, so shall we sleep,
But if it is not, for it is not,
Whose will be the mistake?
Mine, or yours?"

Casimiro Cunhia † 1914
O engano

As vezes diz a Ciência
Que a crença é engano profundo,
Esperando uma outra vida
Noutros planos, noutro mundo...

E diz arrogante à Fé:

– "Estás louca! A morte apenas
É o sono eterno e tranqüilo
Depois das lutas terrenas."

Ao que ela replica, humilde:

– "Mais tarde, Ciência amiga,
Serás o sósia da Fé,
Andarás ao lado meu.
Se for sono, dormiremos,
Mas se não for, pois não é,
De quem será esse engano?
Será meu ou será teu?"

* 1884 Augusto dos Anjos
Human Voice

One voice. Two Voices. Other voices.
Millions of voices. Cosmopolitism.
The yells of beats berserk,
Howling, subdued and ferocious.

It is the human voice, in interminable insanities,
Whether in the thoughts of atheisms,
Or bound to gnosticisms
In their cruel hiccups, coming before death.

It's in this endless painful supplication
I see pain in pleasure, unfulfilled,
Feeding on starving pleasures.

Pain, laughing in our suffering,
Is the worker that weaves the splendors
Of the thorough evolution of all beings.

Augusto dos Anjos † 1914
Voz humana

Uma voz. Duas vozes. Outras vozes.
Milhões de vozes. Cosmopolitismos.
Gritos de feras em paroxismos,
Uivando subjugadas e ferozes.

É a voz humana em intérminas nevroses,
Seja nas concepções dos ateísmos,
Ou mesmo vinculada a gnosticismos
Nos singultos preagônicos, atrozes.

É nessa eterna súplica angustiada
Que eu vejo a dor em gozos, insaciada,
Nutrir-se de famélicos prazeres.

A dor, que gargalhando em nossas dores,
É a obreira que tece os esplendores
Da evolução onímoda dos seres.

* 1872 Batista Celepos
Sonnets

I

One day, I went to Nature and asked,
That it console me of all pains;
Dismayed and sadden, I felt it
As tired and unhappy as all sufferers.

I walked to the doors of Agony,
Eroded from inward burdens,
Looking for the death that seemed to me
Like the ringed end of pains.

Unveiling this tragic secret
That the soul, pale with fear, deciphers
With angst and the fear of the condemned…

But ah! What atrocious remorse pursues me!
I cry, and sob, and clamor and it follows
Into this abyss that opens beneath my feet.

Batista Celepos † 1915
Sonetos

I
Eu fui pedir à Natureza, um dia,
Que me desse um consolo a tantas dores;
Desalentado e triste, pressenti-a
Cansada e triste como os sofredores.

Encaminhei-me à porta da Agonia,
Corroído por chagas interiores,
Buscando a morte que me aparecia
Como o termo anelado aos dissabores,

Desvendando esse trágico segredo
Que a alma decifra, pávida de medo,
Com ansiedade e temores dos galés...

Mas ah! que atroz remorso me persegue!
Choro, soluço, clamo e ele me segue
Nesse abismo que se abre ante os meus pés.

II

No one on Earth hears this lament
Of my vast, uncomprehended grief,
In the frightening darkness of this life
In which I thought I had found Oblivion.

Dark, this endless night,
Full of tempests and suffering,
In the country of dread and suffering,
Where my blinded soul does weep.

Where is non-being, the calm and restful peace,
That would bring balm to this sorrow
Endless, rude, painful?

No one! Not one single voice responds!
I feel only the darkness that conceals me
In the vast of the stormy night…

III

May it serve you as warning, the pain I bring
In my hapless, suffering soul,
This sickening with which I pay
For wondering from the road of salvation.

Here I am only shielded by the vague
Feeling of a new dawn,
When I will have the blessings and soft caress
Of light, that lives in the healing pain.

II
Ninguém ouve na Terra esse lamento
Da minha dor imensa, incompreendida,
Nas pavorosas trevas desta vida
Em que eu julgava achar o Esquecimento.

Tenebrosa, essa noite indefinida,
Cheia de tempestade e sofrimento,
No país do Pavor e do Tormento
Onde chora a minhalma enceguecida.

Onde o não-ser, a paz calma e serena,
Que me traria o bálsamo a esta pena
Interminável, rude, dolorosa?

Ninguém! Uma só voz não me responde!
Sinto somente a treva que me esconde
Na vastidão da noite tormentosa...

III
Sirva-vos de escarmento a dor que trago
Na minhalma infeliz e sofredora,
Este padecimento com que pago
O desvio da estrada salvadora.

Aqui somente ampara-me esse vago
Pressentimento de uma nova aurora,
Quando terei os bens, o brando afago
Da Luz, que está na dor depuradora.

So now, onwards! After so many years
Of torment, amidst the disillusions,
I await the sun of new dawns

Of existences of weeping and toil,
To drink from the chalice of matter
The essences of renounced sorrows!

Agora, sim! depois de tantos anos
De tormentos, em meio aos desenganos,
Espero o sol de novas alvoradas

De existências de pranto e de miséria,
Para beber no cálix da matéria
As essências das dores renegadas!

* 1859   B. Lopes
         Heavenly Sightings

I

Sublime atmospheres,
Shining, rarefied,
Absent the narrow dimensions
Of the hours that measure ages.

And the chosen, pure souls,
Like spring flowers,
Looking in vain for the spheres
Of perfect bliss.

They go, all of them, out in space,
Dawn colored lilies,
Shaped by pain.

And where they pass smiling,
Springing roses blossom,
Roses of peace, and of love.

B. Lopes † 1916
Miragens celestes

I

Sublimes atmosferas,
Luminosas, rarefeitas,
Sem as medidas estreitas
Das horas que marcam eras.

E as almas puras, eleitas,
Quais flores das primaveras,
Buscando vão as esferas
Das alegrias perfeitas.

Vão todas, espaço em fora,
Como lírios cor da aurora,
Modeladas pela dor.

E onde passam sorridentes
Abrem-se rosas virentes,
Rosas de paz e de amor.

II
A meadow of flowers
In broad, infinite space,
Where awakens a foretelling
Of a nightmare of pains.

Wore the robes
Of pleading sufferers,
Lived among the bitter
Of a holy anguish.

And in this ghostly meadow
Received the holy pittance,
In this baptism of light:

Receiving among other joys,
From the lips of shapely angels,
The loving kiss of Jesus.

II
Uma campina de flores
Em pleno espaço infinito,
Onde desperta um precito
De um pesadelo de dores.

Envergara o sambenito
Dos pedintes sofredores,
Vivera entre os amargores
De um sofrimento bendito.

E nessa etérea campina
Recebe a esmola divina,
Nesse batismo de luz;

Recebendo entre outros gozos,
Dos lábios de anjos formosos,
O ósculo de Jesus.

* 1865 Olavo Bilac
Sonnet

I have walked starved and errant for so long,
That the pleasures of this life I have turned into
Poems regarding shapes, in dark
Nightmares of quivering flesh.

In the final dream, moment by moment,
I watched yearnings unweave like cloth
Of illusions turned to cold breath,
Over my fevered chest, wavering.

Death, at your door the soul fumbles,
Peeks, wonders, probes and weeps, full
Of the uncertainty of the sphinx you shape!…

Immovable, you unchain for the distressed
A vision of endless worlds
And an endless watch of ghosts.

Olavo Bilac † 1918
Soneto

Por tanto tempo andei faminto e errante,
Que os prazeres da vida converti-os
Em poemas das formas, em sombrios
Pesadelos da carne palpitante.

No derradeiro sono, instante a instante,
Vi fanarem-se anseios como fios
De ilusão transformada em sopros frios,
Sobre o meu peito em febre, vacilante.

Morte, no teu portal a alma tateia,
Espia, inquire, sonda e chora, cheia
De incerteza na esfinge que tu plasmas!...

Impassível, descerras aos aflitos
Uma visão de mundos infinitos
E uma ronda infinita de fantasmas.

* 1866   Emílio de Menezes
         To My Friends on Earth

Friends, bear my topic,
(I have always lived off other's pains)
Forgive, for the promises of a corpse
Are still uncommon things among you.

Despite my senseless brain,
The bond that did unite us, I have kept,
Like almost longing for the ham,
That feeds a stuffed and ugly body.

I wait for you here with my parties,
In which, however, the wine does not flow,
There is no smell of meats or onions.

Avoid the heavy foods,
For when the "every man for himself" time comes,
Many cannot even keep their trousers…

Emílio de Menezes † 1918
Aos meus amigos da Terra

Amigos, tolerai o meu assunto,
(Sempre vivi do sofrimento alheio)
Relevai, que as promessas de um defunto
São coisa inda invulgar no vosso meio.

Apesar do meu cérebro bestunto,
O elo que nos unia, conservei-o,
Como a quase saudade do presunto,
Que nutre um corpo empanturrado e feio.

Espero-vos aqui com as minhas festas,
Nas quais, porém, o vinho não explode,
Nem há cheiro de carnes ou cebolas.

Evitai as comidas indigestas,
Pois na hora do "salva-se quem pode",
Muita gente nem fica de ceroulas...

* 1877 Luiz Pistarini
In the Strange Portal

At the last instant, the painful tear
Contains the aches of the whole existence,
And the longing is the sad messenger
That adorns with angst, the farewell.

The foresight of the end of all life
Darkens the last visions
And the dark night stretches to the edge
Of the high and abandoned hope.

A blow… A dream… and the high clarinet
Announces other renewed life,
Shining beyond the shadowy tombstone.

It's blown out, the transitory lantern
And the truth shines bright, wrapped in glory,
To the immortal glares of the New Day.

Luiz Pistarini † 1918
No estranho portal

No último instante, a lágrima dorida
Resume as ânsias da existência inteira,
E a saudade é a tristonha mensageira
Que engrinalda de angústia a despedida.

A antevisão do fim de toda a vida
Obscurece a tela derradeira
E a noite escura se distende à beira
Da suprema esperança desvalida.

Um golpe... Um sonho... e excelsa clarinada
Anuncia outra vida renovada,
Brilhando além da lápide sombria.

Apagou-se a candeia transitória
E a verdade refulge envolta em glória,
Aos clarões imortais do Novo Dia.

* 1870 Alphonsus de Guimarãens
To Believers

Oh, believers of another life,
That walk the world exiled,
On the foggy pathways,
Reading the prayer book of bitterness!

Await thy grave,
Oh, believers of another life!...

Sound out the harps of hope,
In the struggles of thy place,
For Death is spring,
Shining, eternal, and immense...

Sons of peace and of belief
Sound out the harps of hope!...

Alphonsus de Guimarãens † 1921
Aos crentes

Ó crentes de uma outra vida,
Que andais no mundo exilados,
Nos caminhos enevoados,
Lendo o missal da amargura!

Esperai a sepultura,
Ó crentes de uma outra vida! ...

Tangei harpas de esperança,
Nas lutas de vossa esfera,
Porque a Morte é a primavera
Luminosa, eterna e imensa...

Filhos da paz e da crença
Tangei harpas de esperança!...

* 1850 Guerra Junqueiro
Eternal Victim

In the silent peace of the top of the Calvary
One can still see, on the cross, the lonely Christ.

Twenty centuries of pain, of cries and agony,
Dammed within the gaze of Mary's Son.

Abandoned and alone in the dryness of the hill
The holy victim suffers endless toil;

Beaten, betrayed, calm and silent,
From Earth to Heaven reaches his merciful gaze.

Two thousand years of pain, and his cruel torturers
Came and went ceaselessly like vicious jackals.

Caravans of kings in passing thrones,
Exalted in the warriors trumpet's voices;

The legendary heroes on horseback,
Writing in fire the maxims of the law.

Gentle knights, blazon-wearing braves,
Blue-blooded nobles on golden mantles.

Guerra Junqueiro † 1923
Eterna vítima

Na silenciosa paz do cimo do Calvário
Ainda se vê na cruz o Cristo solitário.

Vinte séculos de dor, de pranto e de agonia,
Represam-se no olhar do Filho de Maria.

Abandonado e só na aridez da colina
Sofre infindo martírio a vítima divina;

Açoitado, traído e calmo, silencioso,
Da Terra ao Céu espraia o seu olhar piedoso.

Dois mil anos de dor, e os seus cruéis algozes
Passaram sem cessar como chacais ferozes.

Caravanas de reis nos tronos passageiros,
Exaltados na voz das trompas dos guerreiros;

Os lendários heróis no dorso dos corcéis,
Inscrevendo com fogo as máximas das leis.

Cavalheiros gentis, valentes brasonados,
Nobres de sangue azul nos seus mantos dourados.

All saw him bloody, and half-naked, on the cross,
And laughed at the supplicant mad man.

The Christ continued, silent and humble,
Extending over Earth his merciful gaze.

Wise men of old times opening holy books,
Gaze at him too, and cared as little as so many.

Artists and actors, poets and troubadours,
Young lords, hordes of jesters

Still came; then those who, in his name
Spread darkness, weeping, war and famine.

Desolation and horror, brothers killed each other,
Wolves, tigers, jackals, in the cloak of Christians.

Contemplated Jesus at the top of the hill,
Multiplying war, struggle and massacre.

The Master kept going, silent and sublime,
Extending over Earth his merciful gaze.

And in current times the strange caravan
Breaks ground at the foot of the arid mountain;

Though the proud kings and caesars of old,
Are nothing more than miserable beggars, today;

Viram-no seminu, na cruz, ensangüentado,
E puseram-se a rir do louco supliciado!

O Cristo continuou, humilde e silencioso,
Espraiando na Terra o seu olhar piedoso.

Sábios do tempo antigo abrindo os livros santos
Olharam-no também, partindo como tantos.

Artistas e histriões, poetas e trovadores,
Castelãs juvenis, turbas de gozadores

Inda vieram; depois, aqueles que em seu nome
Espalharam a treva, o pranto, a guerra e a fome.

Desolação e horror, mataram-se os irmãos,
Lobos, tigres, chacais, na capa dos cristãos.

Contemplaram Jesus no cume da colina,
Multiplicando a guerra, as lutas e a chacina.

O Mestre prosseguiu, sublime e silencioso,
Espraiando na Terra o seu olhar piedoso.

E na época atual a caravana estranha
Estaca no sopé da árida montanha;

Mas os soberbos reis e césares antigos,
Hoje mais nada são que míseros mendigos;

The noblemen of other times, now changed
Into pariahs of bitterness, of the greatly damned,

Now see, yes, at the top of the Calvary,
The sacrifice and pain of the eternal visionary,

Howling in rage: – "Save us, Jesus!
That we may defeat the pain of our crosses.

For in tasting the bitter gall in the pains of affliction,
One is hungry for peace and thirsty for forgiveness!"

And the Master of kindness, the angel of virtue,
Extends his forgiveness full of appeasement.

And from atop the cross, silent and calm,
Consoles the crowds with his merciful gaze.

Os nobres doutro tempo, agora transformados
Nos párias do amargor, nos grandes desgraçados,

Agora vêem, sim, no topo do Calvário,
O sacrifício e a dor do eterno visionário,

Bradando com furor: – "Socorre-nos Jesus!
Que possamos vencer a dor em nossa cruz.

Sorvendo o amaro fel nas dores da aflição,
Temos fome de paz e sede de perdão!"

E o Mestre da bondade, o anjo da virtude,
Estende o seu perdão cheio de mansuetude.

E do cimo da cruz, calmo e silencioso,
Consola a multidão com o seu olhar piedoso.

* 1885 Amaral Ornellas
Ave Maria

Ave Maria! Lady
Of love, supporting, redeeming,
Woe of the world if not for
Thy lofty quest!

Full of grace and kindness,
'Tis through thee that we may know
The eternal revelation
Of life in its supreme gifts.

Our Lord is always with thee,
Message of tenderness,
Providence for the weeping
In the shadows of misadventures.

Blessed art thou, oh Queen!
Star of Humanity,
Mystic rose of faith,
Pure lily of humility!

Amaral Ornellas † 1923
Ave Maria

Ave Maria! Senhora
Do Amor que ampara e redime,
Ai do mundo se não fora
A vossa missão sublime!

Cheia de graça e bondade,
É por vós que conhecemos
A eterna revelação
Da vida em seus dons supremos.

O Senhor sempre é convosco,
Mensageira da ternura,
Providência dos que choram
Nas sombras da desventura.

Bendita sois vós, Rainha!
Estrela da Humanidade,
Rosa mística da fé,
Lírio puro da humildade!

Among women art thou
The Mother of helpless mothers,
Our door of hope,
And Angel of our lives!

Blessed is the immortal fruit
Of thy quest of light,
From the peace of the Manger,
To the pains, beyond the Cross.

Thus may it always be,
Oh! Divine Sovereign,
Refuge for the weary
Of the pains of human struggle.

Ave Maria! Lady
Of love, supporting, redeeming,
Woe of the world if not for
Thy lofty quest!

Entre as mulheres sois vós
A Mãe das mães desvalidas,
Nossa porta de esperança,
E Anjo de nossas vidas!

Bendito o fruto imortal
Da vossa missão de luz,
Desde a paz da Manjedoura,
Às dores, além da Cruz.

Assim seja para sempre,
Oh! Divina Soberana,
Refúgio dos que padecem
Nas dores da luta humana.

Ave Maria! Senhora
Do Amor que ampara e redime,
Ai do mundo se não fora
A vossa missão sublime!

* 1856 Múcio Teixeira
Honor to Work

Work, and you shall find the diamond thread
That binds you to the Lord who guards and rules us,
Before whose greatness the world bows,
Seeking the solution for pain and fate.

From the sun's base to the cave's depths,
From the hero's beauty to the small worm,
Everything rattles and shakes, in holy chant
Of the immortal work, making bright, the eternal life!…

Everything in the immensity is lavish service,
Joyous to help, in struggle and contentment,
From the mountain flower to the granite's darkness.

Work and serve always, with no mind to reward,
That the work, for itself, is the glory that brings together
The means of the Earth and the blessing of the Infinite.

Múcio Teixeira † 1926
Honra ao trabalho

Trabalha e encontrarás o fio diamantino
Que te liga ao Senhor que nos guarda e governa,
Ante cuja grandeza o mundo se prosterna,
Buscando a solução da dor e do destino.

Desde o fulcro solar ao fundo da caverna,
Da beleza do herói ao verme pequenino,
Tudo se agita e vibra, em cântico divino
Do trabalho imortal, brunindo a vida eterna!...

Tudo na imensidão é serviço opulento,
Júbilo de ajudar, luta e contentamento,
Desde a flor da montanha às trevas do granito.

Trabalha e serve sempre, alheio à recompensa,
Que o trabalho, por si, é a glória que condensa
O salário da Terra e a bênção do Infinito.

* 1895 Raul de Leoni
We...

We all go throughout life
Leaving on the path the same traces,
In God searching for the Perfection that lives
On the unreachable summit of Spaces!...

Each instant of pain improves us,
Unbinding the shackles, breaking the bonds
Of this delaying animosity,
That seeks to hamper our stride.

Heroes of new Carolingian myths
The dream binds our souls, girdles them,
In the Ideal Light – our highest shield;

Searching for the Ineffable, the Unfathomed,
God, which is eternal boundless Love
And the glorious synthesis of all.

Raul de Leoni † 1926
Nós...

Nós todos vamos pela vida em fora
Deixando no caminho os mesmos traços,
Em Deus buscando a Perfeição que mora
No cume inatingível dos Espaços!...

Cada instante de dor nos aprimora,
Desatando os grilhões, rompendo os laços
Dessa animalidade atrasadora,
Que procura tolher os nossos passos.

Heróis de novas lendas carlovíngias,
O Sonho imanta as nossas almas, cinge-as,
Na Luz Ideal – o nosso excelso escudo;

Buscando o Indefinível, o Insondado,
Deus, que é o Amor eterno e ilimitado
E a gloriosa síntese de tudo.

* 1899 Rodrigues de Abreu
Saw Thee, Lord!

I could not see Thee, my Lord,
In the well-ventured of the world,
Like the humble and faithful man in Tolstoy's tale.

I could never see
Thy soft and merciful hands,
Where Earth's aches and miseries moan;
And the truth, Lord,
Is that I would find Thee, as Thou still art,
In the rougher more thorny ways,
Consoling the stricken and the desperate…
Thou art in the temple of all religions,
Where they search for Thy affection
These suffering souls,
Mistaking those who spill the poison of hate in Thy name,
Bringing the sweet sight on Heaven
To the weary eyes of all hopes…
Thou art in the direction of men,
In all the paths of their earthly trades,
Without their knowledge
Of Thy silent and renewing word,
Of Thy mighty and invisible aid,
Full of mercy for their weaknesses.

Rodrigues de Abreu † 1927
Vi-te, Senhor!

Eu não pude ver-Te, meu Senhor,
Nos bem-aventurados do mundo,
Como aquele homem humilde e crente do conto de Tolstoi.

Nunca pude enxergar
As Tuas mãos suaves e misericordiosas,
Onde gemiam as dores e as misérias da Terra;
E a verdade, Senhor,
É que Te achavas, como ainda Te encontras,
Nos caminhos mais rudes e espinhosos,
Consolando os aflitos e os desesperados...
Estás no templo de todas as religiões,
Onde busquem Teus carinhos
As almas sofredoras,
Confundindo os que lançam o veneno do ódio em Teu nome,
Trazendo a visão doce do Céu
Para o olhar angustioso de todas as esperanças.
Estás na direção dos homens,
Em todos os caminhos de suas atividades terrestres,
Sem que eles se apercebam
De Tua palavra silenciosa e renovadora,
De Tua assistência invisível e poderosa,
Cheia de piedade para com as suas fraquezas.

Still,
I was also blind among the wiggling worms that are men,
And did not find Thee over rough roads…

Youth, joy, dream and love,
Ambitious restlessness to win,
And my life rolled down the slope of all troubles.

Thou called me, though,
With the softness of Thy infinite mercy.
Not by name, so as not to offend me;
Called me without weepy proclamations,
With the silent verb of Thy love,
And before death crowned Thy kindness towards me,
I saw Thee slowly coming near,
Illuminating the sanctuary of my thoughts
With Thy perennial light!

You spoke with me with Thy language from the Sermon on
                                          the Mound,
And multiplied the bread of my joys
And opened up Heaven, that the Earth closed inside my soul…

And I understood Thee, Lord,
In Thy wonders of beauty,
When I saw Thee in the peace of Nature,
Healing me with Pain.

Entretanto,
Eu era também cego no meio dos vermes vibráteis que são os homens,
E não Te encontrava pelos caminhos ásperos...

Mocidade, alegria, sonho e amor,
Inquietação ambiciosa de vencer,
E minha vida rolava no declive de todas as ânsias...

Chamaste-me, porém,
Com a mansidão de Tua misericórdia infinita.
Não disseste o meu nome para não me ofender;
Chamaste-me sem exclamações lamentosas,
Com o verbo silencioso do Teu amor,
E antes que a morte coroasse a Tua magnanimidade para comigo,
Vi que chegavas devagarinho,
Iluminando o santuário do meu pensamento
Com a Tua luz de todos os séculos!

Falaste-me com a Tua linguagem do Sermão da Montanha,
Multiplicaste o pão das minhas alegrias
E abriste-me o Céu, que a Terra fechara dentro de minhalma...

E entendi-Te, Senhor,
Nas Tuas maravilhas de beleza,
Quando Te vi na paz da Natureza,
Curando-me com a Dor.

*1861 Luís Murat
Even Beyond…

You wanderer who, at day's end,
Demands the twilight of your aches,
Do not lose yourself in the shadowy tear
Of the torment of yearnings and bitterness!

Beyond the grave begins
The path of redeeming dreams,
In the perpetual dawn of harmony,
Adorned with eternal splendors.

Desolate traveler, open your eyes!
Do not hold yourself to bleak ground,
Keep the sweet and lovely hope!

Conquer the long journey of thorns,
That the shining country of your dream
Is up high… distant… even beyond…

Luís Murat † 1929
Além ainda…

Caminheiro que vais ao fim do dia
Demandando o crepúsculo das dores,
Não te percas na lágrima sombria
Da tormenta de anseios e amargores!

Além da sepultura principia
O caminho dos sonhos redentores,
Na alvorada perene da harmonia,
Aureolada de eternos resplendores.

Desolado viajor, ergue teus olhos!
Não te prendas somente ao chão tristonho,
Guarda a esperança carinhosa e linda!

Vence a longa jornada dos abrolhos,
Que o país luminoso do teu sonho
Fica ao alto… distante… além ainda…

*1871 Valado Rosas
To My Brothers

Under the stars of my belief,
Tired and weary I shut my eyes
Inside the night that is for many
A stormy sea, full of hurdles.

When in the world of exile and shadow,
I grew accustomed to the winter
And turnabouts of my own luck,
In the hard struggle that filled my days,

It's then that the Gospel of beloved Christ,
– The messenger of Perfection,
In the sad and bitter hours,
Clears my heart.

I am not, however, the one to show
The wonders it provides,
When we hear the clear voices
Of consciousness, in the light of prayer.

Valado Rosas † 1930
Aos meus irmãos

Sob as estrelas da minha crença,
Cansado e triste cerrei meus olhos
Dentro da noite que é para muitos
Um mar bravio, cheio de escolhos.

Quando no mundo de exílio e sombra,
Habituei-me com as invernias
E com os reveses da minha sorte,
Na luta intensa que encheu meus dias,

É que o Evangelho do Cristo amado,
– O mensageiro da Perfeição,
Nas horas tristes e amarguradas,
Esclarecia meu coração.

Não sou, no entanto, quem vá mostrar
As maravilhas que ele fornece,
Quando escutamos as vozes claras
Da consciência, na luz da prece.

And, so, I could fall asleep
In the sweet, serene and Christian peace,
Opening my eyes calmly
In a high and beautiful dawn.

You, who have stayed behind in the ungrateful world,
Of whom I remember, in the light of the Beyond,
Read the script of the Gospels…
And peace in death, you shall have as well.

E, então, eu pude adormecer
Na paz serena, doce e cristã,
Abrindo os olhos tranqüilamente
Numa alvorada linda e louçã.

Vós, que ficastes no mundo ingrato,
De quem me lembro na luz do Além,
Lede o roteiro dos Evangelhos...
E a paz na morte tereis também.

* 1888　Hermes Fontes
Sonnet

I am the farmhand, rough and untrained,
Who's done the rare and shining sowing
Of the blond wheat and the wonder of the dream…
– Beautiful dream without equal.

He did not notice the sad and dreary toil,
Drenched, in crying, the land he farmed;
With naive soul and laughing heart,
Waited, certain, for the sun on the field.

And after the work and the torment,
While waiting, joyous, for the reaping,
In greatly disappointed hope,

Lo, there came devastations,
And the poor, miserable and miss-adventured,
Lost it all, at the moment of the harvest.

Hermes Fontes † 1930
Soneto

Sou, o lavrador que fez, rude e bisonho,
A sementeira luminosa e rara
Do trigo louro e rútilo do sonho...
– Sonho lindo que a nada se compara.

Não reparou o labor triste e enfadonho,
Regou, chorando, a terra que lavrara;
E de alma ingênua e coração risonho,
Esperou confiante o sol da seara.

Passados os trabalhos e os tormentos,
Quando aguardava a messe, jubiloso,
Numa grande esperança insatisfeita,

Eis que aparecem os arrasamentos,
E o pobre, desgraçado e desditoso,
Perdeu tudo no instante da colheita.

* 1838 Juvenal Galeno
From Here

How bitter was my fate!…
Sadness in the heart,
Grabbling awkwardly
In the midst of darkness…

To live on Earth and only
Paddle against the tide,
Afraid of hitting bottom…
Is surely no great thing.

This life of suffering
For thirty days each month,
Mingled in weeping,
Is there one who would esteem it? Perhaps…

But for me, who was ever only
A Galeno without purpose, a slave,
So many pains put together,
Is surely no great thing.

Juvenal Galeno † 1931
De cá

Que amargo era o meu destino!...
Tristezas no coração,
Tateando dificilmente
No meio da escuridão...

Viver na Terra e somente
Remando contra a maré,
Com receio de ir ao fundo...
Nem tão boa coisa é.

Esta vida de sofrer
Trinta dias cada mês,
Entremeados de prantos,
Há quem estime? Talvez...

Mas para mim que só fui,
Galeno sem nó, galé,
Tantas dores em conjunto,
Nem tão boa coisa é.

To feel the injustices
Of lives full of pain,
Evil choking the world,
And marching fearless:

To see the rich man riding carriages
And the poor man running on foot,
To feel so many miseries…
Is surely no great thing.

Weeping boils up from the Earth,
Springs out here, springs out there,
In the wars of everywhere,
In the drought of Ceará;

My brothers from Fortaleza,
From Crato, from Canindé,
To see some laughing while others weep,
Is surely no great thing.

Ah! To die and yet to feel
Such longing for slavery,
For flesh, for discomfort,
For darkness, for ingratitude…

It is not possible,
My poor son of the riffraff,
Because to marry misfortune,
Is surely no great thing.

Sentir as disparidades
Das vidas cheias de dor,
O mal sufocando o mundo,
Marchando com destemor:

Ver o rico andar de coche
E o pobre correndo a pé,
Tantas misérias sentir...
Nem tão boa coisa é.

O pranto ferve na Terra,
Salta aqui, salta acolá,
Nas guerras de toda parte,
Nas secas do Ceará;

Meus irmãos de Fortaleza,
Do Crato, do Canindé,
Ver uns rindo e outros chorando,
Nem tão boa coisa é.

Ah! morrer e ainda sentir
Saudades da escravidão,
Da carne, do desconforto,
Da treva, da ingratidão...

Não é possível porque,
Pobre filho da ralé,
Casar-se com a desventura
Nem tão boa coisa é.

But to speak too much now,
Is not at all like me,
And I will not waste my wax
With the dead rabble;

Foolish is it to teach
Truth to faithless men.
Throwing pearls before fools,
Is surely no great thing.

Mas falar demais agora,
Já não é próprio de mim,
Não vou gastar minha cera
Com tanto defunto ruim;

Patetice é ensinar
Verdade aos homens sem fé.
Jogar pérolas a tolos,
Nem tão boa coisa é.

* 1859 José Silvério Horta
Prayer

Our Father, who art in Heaven,
In the light of endless suns,
Father of all of the troubled
Of this world of turmoil.

Hallowed, Lord,
Be thy sublime name,
That in all the Universe expounds
Harmony, tenderness and love.

Come to our heart
Thy kingdom of kindness,
Of peace and clarity
On the road of redemption.

Fulfilled, may thy commandment be
That which does not waver or miss,
In Heaven, as it is on all the Earth
Of struggle and suffering.

José Silvério Horta † 1933
Oração

Pai Nosso, que estás nos Céus,
Na luz dos sóis infinitos,
Pai de todos os aflitos
Deste mundo de escarcéus.

Santificado, Senhor,
Seja o teu nome sublime,
Que em todo o Universo exprime
Concórdia, ternura e amor.

Venha ao nosso coração
O teu reino de bondade,
De paz e de claridade
Na estrada da redenção.

Cumpra-se o teu mandamento
Que não vacila e nem erra,
Nos Céus, como em toda a Terra
De luta e de sofrimento.

Avoid for us all evil,
Give us the bread on the way,
Made in the light, in the care
Of the spiritual bread.

Forgive us, my Lord,
The dark debts,
Of rough pasts,
Of inequality and pain.

Help us, too,
In Christian sentiment,
To love our brothers
That live far from the good.

With the protection of Jesus,
Deliver our soul of error,
On this world of banishment,
Far from your light.

That our ideal church
Be the altar of Charity,
Where it be done the will
Of your love… May it be so.

Evita-nos todo o mal,
Dá-nos o pão no caminho,
Feito na luz, no carinho
Do pão espiritual.

Perdoa-nos, meu Senhor,
Os débitos tenebrosos,
De passados escabrosos,
De iniqüidade e de dor.

Auxilia-nos, também,
Nos sentimentos cristãos,
A amar nossos irmãos
Que vivem longe do bem.

Com a proteção de Jesus,
Livra a nossa alma do erro,
Sobre o mundo de desterro,
Distante da vossa luz.

Que a nossa ideal igreja
Seja o altar da Caridade,
Onde se faça a vontade
Do vosso amor... Assim seja.

* 1902 Cármen Cinira
The Traveler and Faith

– "Whence do you come, sad and weary traveler?"
– "I come from the barren land of illusion."
– "What do you bring?"
– "The misery of sin.
Of dead heart and wounded soul.
Ah! How I wish for the blessing of hope,
And for the solace from misfortune!"

But the soft, humble and generous faith,
Held him and spoke with kindness:
– "Come to the Master that soothes the poor ones,
That enlightens and comforts those who suffer!…
For with the world, a flower has a thousand thorns,
But with Jesus, a thorn has a thousand flowers!"

Cármen Cinira † 1933
O viajor e a Fé

– "Donde vens, viajor triste e cansado?"
– "Venho da terra estéril da ilusão."
– "Que trazes?"
– "A miséria do pecado,
De alma ferida e morto o coração.
Ah! quem me dera a bênção da esperança,
Quem me dera consolo à desventura!"

Mas a fé generosa, humilde e mansa,
Deu-lhe o braço e falou-lhe com doçura:
– "Vem ao Mestre que ampara os pobrezinhos,
Que esclarece e conforta os sofredores!...
Pois com o mundo uma flor tem mil espinhos,
Mas com Jesus um espinho tem mil flores!"

* 1877 Abel Gomes
We Have Jesus

In dark mirk the Old World collapses
And the war, like a meat-loving wolf,
Threatens truth and humbles faith,
In the tortures of a new captivity.

But thou, in the whirlwind of the great shadow,
Hast with thee the High Companion,
That loves the labor and forgets reward
In the service of good to the entire world.

Thus, it is that Earth has crimes and tyrants,
Ambitions, madnesses, disillusions,
And the coarseness of cavemen;

But thou hast Jesus in each day.
Let us labor in pain or joy,
And gain the light of Eternal Life.

Abel Gomes † 1934
Temos Jesus

Desaba o Velho Mundo em treva densa
E a guerra, como lobo carniceiro,
Ameaça a verdade e humilha a crença,
Nas torturas de um novo cativeiro.

Mas vós, no turbilhão da sombra imensa,
Tendes convosco o Excelso Companheiro,
Que ama o trabalho e esquece a recompensa
No serviço do bem ao mundo inteiro.

Eis que a Terra tem crimes e tiranos,
Ambições, desvarios, desenganos,
Asperezas dos homens da caverna;

Mas vós tendes Jesus em cada dia.
Trabalhemos na dor ou na alegria,
Na conquista de luz da Vida Eterna.

*1885 Antônio Torres
Ship of Dreams

I had a dream of love and innocence,
Full of the light of treasured things,
From which I lost the shining core
In the awakening of my woes.

Late, did I acknowledge my faults,
And after the many tragedies,
Of my nearly useless existence,
In the silence of buried ashes.

And to Death, in the nameless abyss,
I fell into, spent, bitter and blind,
– Fearsome abyss, which I transpose.

Hapless is my wasted being,
For sad and dizzy, I still carry
The black ship of my own dream.

Antônio Torres † 1934
Esquife do sonho

Tive um sonho de amor e de inocência,
Cheio de luz das coisas invulgares,
Do qual perdi a luminosa essência
Na cristalização dos meus pesares.

Tarde reconheci minha falência,
Terminados os múltiplos azares,
De minha quase inútil existência,
No silêncio das cinzas tumulares.

E da morte, no abismo indefinido,
Tombei exausto, amargurado e cego,
– Abismo tenebroso que eu transponho.

Infeliz do meu ser irredimido,
Pois triste e atordoado inda carrego
O negro esquife do meu próprio sonho.

* 1870 Alberto de Oliveira
Jesus

How often, in this world, on pathways dark and uncertain,
Man feels around the dark in which he dwells!
Around, all is vain, on the dark road,
In the fright of awaiting the coming angst!…

Between the throes of death, chest clean and open,
Damned traveler, rebel to its guide,
Desperate, sobs, yearns and rants
A supreme prayer of pain from his desert.

In this great bitterness, the poor soul, among wreckage,
Feels the Master of Love that shows him, amidst debris,
The greatness of the cross that shines and helps;

From the world is the darkness, which buries the chimera…
And in the dark volcano only Jesus remains,
Like the immortal light of love undying.

Alberto de Oliveira † 1937
Jesus

Quanta vez, neste mundo, em rumo escuro e incerto,
O homem vive a tatear na treva em que se cria!
Em torno, tudo é vão, sobre a estrada sombria,
No pavor de esperar a angústia que vem perto!...

Entre as vascas da morte, o peito exangue e aberto,
Desgraçado viajor rebelado ao seu guia,
Desespera, soluça, anseia e balbucia
A suprema oração da dor do seu deserto.

Nessa grande amargura, a alma pobre, entre escombros,
Sente o Mestre do Amor que lhe mostra nos ombros
A grandeza da cruz que ilumina e socorre;

Do mundo é a escuridão, que sepulta a quimera...
E no escuro bulcão só Jesus persevera,
Como a luz imortal do amor que nunca morre.

* 1870 Belmiro Braga
Verses from Another World

I

I've arrived happily at my port,
I am younger and stronger,
Found peace and comfort
In life, after dying.
Here are the rhymes of another north,
That the dead poet writes.

II

With arrogant ignorance,
That death is the end, man thinks,
Judging from the stem of the weed
The vast and beautiful landscape.
Ah! Happy he that keeps
The sweet lights of belief.

III

How many people run, and run,
Anxiously after pleasure,
Dream and weep, struggle and die
Without ever knowing it.
And there is no one on this Earth,
That can be set free from dying.

Belmiro Braga † 1937
Rimas de Outro Mundo

I
Cheguei feliz ao meu porto,
Estou mais moço e mais forte,
Encontrei paz e conforto
Na vida, depois da morte.
Eis as rimas de outro norte,
Que escreve o poeta morto.

II
Com a ignorância proterva,
Que a morte é o fim, o homem pensa,
Julgando no talo de erva
A paisagem linda e imensa.
Ah! feliz o que conserva
As luzes doces da crença.

III
Quanta gente corre, corre,
Ansiosa atrás do prazer,
Sonha e chora, luta e morre
Sem jamais o conhecer.
Não há ninguém que se forre,
Sobre a Terra, ao padecer.

IV
Close the bag of ambition,
Do not chase after luck,
Worship the hand that extorts you
In the days of trials,
Be brave, my brother,
No one meets his end in death.

V
In this world is worthy he who
May have some silver or gold;
But from the swallowing of death,
No one ever escapes!
In Heaven the only treasure valued
Is from the one whose deeds were good.

VI
That your soul may burn in prayer
In the fire of devotion.
God is a Father who is never late
On the road to grief
And during the heartaches of the world
Keep the faith in your heart.

VII
Between faith and fanaticism,
Many a spirit is mistaken:
The first cares for and stands beside,
The second is dogmatism,

IV
Fecha a bolsa da ambição,
Não corras atrás da sorte,
Venera a mão que te exorte
Nos dias de provação.
Tem coragem, meu irmão,
Ninguém se acaba com a morte.

V
No mundo vale quem tem
Um cifrão de prata ou de ouro;
Mas, da morte ao sorvedouro,
Jamais escapa ninguém!
No Céu só vale o tesouro
Daquele que fez o bem.

VI
Que tua alma em preces arda
No fogo da devoção.
Deus é Pai que nunca tarda
No caminho da aflição.
Nas mágoas do mundo, guarda
A fé do teu coração.

VII
Entre a fé e o fanatismo,
Muito espírito se engana:
A primeira ampara e irmana,
O segundo é o dogmatismo,

The open mouth of an abyss
On the road of human living.

VIII
The Earth is, to those who fell,
Still the tower of Babel,
Where the actual reveals
The illusions of what's on paper:
Many smiles around,
Hearts of sludge and gall.

IX
Bear the pain that covers you
In the evil, thorny road,
The rich, and the noble,
To this road shall return.
It is a venture to be poor,
With the blessings that God grants us.

X
In life, I have always assumed,
Without much thought or philosophy,
That, for the Kingdom of Light,
It would be enough, on the dark Earth,
That men follow Jesus,
That women follow Mary.

Goela aberta de um abismo
Na estrada da vida humana.

VIII
A Terra, para quem sente,
Inda é torre de Babel,
Onde a prática desmente
As ilusões do papel:
Muita boca sorridente,
Corações de lodo e fel.

IX
Suporta a dor que te cobre
Na estrada espinhosa e má,
Quem é rico, quem é nobre,
A essa estrada voltará.
É uma ventura ser pobre,
Com a bênção que Deus nos dá.

X
Na vida sempre supus,
Sem muita filosofia,
Que, em prol do Reino da Luz,
Basta, na Terra sombria,
Que o homem siga a Jesus,
Que a mulher siga a Maria.

* 1881 Gustavo Teixeira
To Saint Peter of Piracicaba

Last instant, final picture
In the long lines of the shadowy processions
It was death, closing my eyelids
At the painful end of the pilgrimage.

Thanks to God, belief was my squire
And seeking, anxiously, the steady hands,
I wept in gratitude as I felt them
Leading me to the light of another landscape.

Oh land of Saint Peter, whom I love so,
With what angst did I see you, bathed in tears,
In my great and sad gasps!…

Work and wait under smiling skies,
For death is life for these dreams of ours,
And paradise for our pains.

Gustavo Teixeira † 1937
A São Pedro de Piracicaba

Último instante, derradeira imagem
Nas procissões da sombra em longas filas...
Era a morte, cerrando-me as pupilas
No doloroso termo da romagem.

Graças a Deus, a crença era meu pajem
E buscando-lhe, ansioso, as mãos tranqüilas,
Chorei de gratidão ao pressenti-las,
Conduzindo-me à luz doutra paisagem.

Ó terra de São Pedro, que amo tanto,
Com que angústias te vi, banhado em pranto,
Nos supremos e tristes estertores!...

Trabalha e espera sob os céus risonhos,
Que a morte é vida para os nossos sonhos,
E paraíso para as nossas dores.

* 1875   Pedro de Alcântra
         Page of Gratitude

Striking the strings of the harp of longing,
I come to Brazil to search for the pure core
Of the love of my country, of the sweetness
Of the flower full of scents of friendship.

Arrest my heart, the softness
Of this rapture of affection and tenderness
Of my people's soul, that from happiness
And joy invades my spirit.

From the mysterious beyond death, I see,
Feeling this bright, forceful wave
Of affection, that captures my wish:

And having gratitude as company,
I return to where I belong with a longing soul,
Loving more, the Brazilian Land.

Pedro de Alcântra † 1940
Página de gratidão

Tangendo as cordas da harpa da saudade,
Venho ao Brasil buscar a essência pura
Do amor da pátria minha, da doçura
Da flor cheia do aroma da amizade.

Prende-me o coração a suavidade
Desse arroubo de afeto e de ternura
D'alma do povo meu, que de ventura
E de alegria o espírito me invade.

Do misterioso aquém da morte, eu vejo,
Sentindo, essa onda intensa e luminosa
Da afeição, que idealiza o meu desejo:

E tendo a gratidão por companheira,
Volvo ao pátrio torrão de alma saudosa,
Amando mais a Terra Brasileira.

* 1865   Albérico Lobo
From My Port

To my dear friend M. Quintão

Wondering, tired traveler,
After crossing the endless shadow,
I have found the blessed country
Where the heavenly prize resides.

Goodbye to the sorrows of the strange, heavy night,
Of anxieties and dreams of past,
Hold nothing but Love and Faith,
Before the boundless new path.

Take sweet rest after toil,
And bathe the heart in the light of life,
Remembering the pains now past...

And for the happy crews from my port,
Pray to Jesus may he grant comfort
To the beloved hearts who stayed!

Albérico Lobo
Do meu porto

† 1942

Ao caro amigo M. Quintão

Viajor vacilante e extenuado,
Depois de atravessar a sombra imensa,
Encontrei o país abençoado
Onde vive a celeste recompensa.

Adeus mágoas da noite estranha e densa,
Das angústias e sonhos do passado,
Não conservo senão o Amor e a Crença,
Ante o novo caminho ilimitado.

É doce descansar após a lida,
Banhar o coração na luz da vida,
Rememorando as dores que passaram...

E dos quadros risonhos do meu porto,
Rogo a Jesus conceda reconforto
Aos corações amados que ficaram!

* 1902 Jesus Gonçalves
Angel of Redemption

From Heaven you descended, shining and pure
And in the holy mystery in which you hide
You dressed me in the robe of rot and wound
And cuffed me to the strange and hard wood.

A solar deity hovering over trash,
Triple, hiding the flowers with which you caress,
You heard me in silence, my crying and my cursing,
Sweet and invisible, in the dark path!...

But, from the cross of wounds that you gave me,
You freed my being to the Heavenly Light,
Where, bright and sublime, you flame!

And now I shout, at last, with hearty soul:
– "God bless you, oh fair and merciful Pain,
Angel of redemption! Be blessed!..."

Jesus Gonçalves † 1947
Anjo de redenção

Do Céu desceste resplendente e puro
E no santo mistério em que te apagas
Vestiste-me o burel de sânie e chagas
E algemaste-me a lenho estranho e duro.

Nume solar pairando no monturo,
Terno, escondendo as flores com que afagas,
Ouviste-me, em silêncio, o choro e as pragas,
Doce e invisível no caminho escuro!...

Mas, da cruz de feridas que me deste,
Libertaste meu ser à Luz Celeste,
Onde, sublime e fúlgido, flamejas!

E agora brado, enfim, de alma robusta:
– "Deus te abençoe, ó Dor piedosa e justa,
Anjo da redenção! bendito sejas!..."

*1881 Alfredo Nora
Speedy Letter

Dear Lasneau, it's not a note,
Not a statement, nor a record.
It is the heart unwinding
My sorrows in a reminder.

I

Lasneau my friend, this shack,
Where the flesh, briefly, passes,
Full of mud and smoke,
Is such a tiny hovel.

The Earth, before the sun of Grace,
Is like a small plowing field,
Holding as our mistakes
Disbelief, war, and cachaça.

It is now that I see this,
But it's sad, faith without its life
That dying makes hurried…

Wait without commotion,
Beyond this jail of bones,
Real life will begin.

Alfredo Nora
Carta ligeira

† 1947

Meu Lasneau, não é bilhete,
Não é ofício, nem ata.
É o coração que desata
Meus pesares num lembrete. 1

|
Lasneau amigo, esta choça,
Onde a carne, breve, passa,
Cheia de lama e fumaça,
É minúscula palhoça.

A Terra, ante o sol da Graça,
É feio talhão de roça,
Detendo por balda nossa
Descrença, guerra e cachaça.

Agora é que entendo isso,
Mas é triste a fé sem viço
Que o sepulcro impõe à pressa...

Espere sem alvoroço,
Além da prisão de osso,
A vida real começa.

II
Oh! My dear, if I could
Say all I did not,
Without the old weirdness,
That still dulls me now!

However, the gain is clear
From the seeds of silliness.
I lost my time in folly
And time now knows me not.

It is natural that it may die
My poor mind
Face to face with the Light.

Do not forget me in your prayer,
I wish your struggle end,
That things may improve and… pass.

II
Oh! meu caro, se eu pudesse
Dizer tudo o que não disse,
Sem a velha esquisitice
Que inda agora me entontece!

Entretanto, é clara a messe
Da sementeira de asnice.
Perdi tempo em maluquice
E o tempo me desconhece.

É natural que padeça
A minha pobre cabeça
Perante a Luz, face a face.

Não me olvide em sua prece,
Desejo que a luta cesse,
Que a coisa melhore e... passe.

* 1865 Leôncio Correia
Longing

Before the brightness of rebirthing life
After the cold, dense, strange fog,
Spring constellations of the New Day
Far from the hapless Earth.

Celestial worlds, kingdoms of joy
And empires of overwhelming beauty
Sing in Space, joyously,
To the rhythm of Love and Harmony…

But, oh! Poor me!… Before the greatness
Of the highest glory shining
I return to deadly shadows of the deep abyss!

And, crushed with anguish and affection,
I weep of love, seeing again the old nest
And the tender birds which I left in the world!…

Leôncio Correia † 1950
Saudade

Ante o brilho da vida renascente
Depois da névoa estranha, densa e fria,
Surgem constelações do Novo Dia
Muito longe da Terra descontente.

Mundos celestes, reinos de alegria
E impérios da beleza resplendente
Cantam no Espaço, jubilosamente,
Ao compasso do Amor e da Harmonia…

Mas, ai! pobre de mim!… Ante a grandeza
Da glória excelsa eternamente acesa
Volvo à sombra letal do abismo fundo!

E, esmagado de angústia e de carinho,
Choro de amor, revendo o velho ninho
E as aves ternas que deixei no mundo!…

A.G.
Death

Silent maiden of sorrow,
Death has opened for me radiant cathedrals
Where hover the vaporous shapes
Of the forgotten land of Beauty.

In a deluge of lilacs and roses,
Sons of light, of another Nature,
That shaped in space the subtlety
Of the incense of luminous ships!

Monk of merciful look, calm and distant,
Brings to Earth the shy humming
Of the mansion of wondering stars…

Sister of peace and serenity,
That opened my eyes to immortality,
To the hope of all my days!

A.G.
Morte

Silenciosa madona da tristeza,
A morte abriu-me as catedrais radiosas,
Onde pairam as formas vaporosas
Do país ignorado da Beleza.

Num dilúvio de lírios e de rosas,
Filhos da luz de uma outra Natureza,
Que entornavam no espaço a sutileza
Dos incensos das naves harmoniosas!

Monja de olhar piedoso, calmo e austero,
Que traz à Terra um tênue reverbero
Da mansão das estrelas erradias...

Irmã da paz e da serenidade,
Que abriu meus olhos na imortalidade,
À esperança de todos os meus dias!

Amadeu
The Mystery of Death

The mystery of death is the mystery of life,
That leaves spent and dying matter;
That brings within, the dark, and opens the golden door
Of a world that amongst us is the unknown light.

I also had, long ago, my soul disturbed,
By doubt, uncertainty and angst consumed,
But death healed the last wound for me
Unweaving the utopic lessons of the Nothing.

Death is nothing but the lucid process,
Dissimilating the forms reachable,
To the light of your gaze, impoverished and unclear.

I come bearing witness to the light from which I return,
Inciting thy soul to the invisible plans,
Where the freed Spirit lives and stretches out.

Amadeu
O mistério da morte

O mistério da morte é o mistério da vida,
Que abandona a matéria exânime e cansada;
Que traz a treva em si e abre a porta dourada
De um mundo que entre nós é a luz desconhecida.

Também tive a minhalma outrora perturbada,
De dúvida, incerteza e angústias consumida,
Mas a morte sanou-me a última ferida
Desfazendo as lições utópicas do Nada.

A morte é simplesmente o lúcido processo
Desassimilador das formas acessíveis
A luz do vosso olhar, empobrecido e incerto.

Venho testemunhar a luz de onde regresso,
Incitando vossa alma aos planos invisíveis,
Onde vive e se expande o Espírito liberto.

Alma Eros
The Chalice

The rain, healthy and plenty, falls from the sky
Mitigating the earth's thirst
And so, alike, the Beloved rains over man
Powers and blessings.
However, you cry and despair…
Why did you not gather in time, your portion?
– Nothing saw I – you answer…
It is because your eyes were hazy in the atmosphere of dreams.

The Lord passes by every day,
Giving out heavenly gifts,
But the hollows of your heart are pouring out with strange
                                                  substances.

Here, you keep the vinegar of disillusions,
There, the poisoned liquor of whims.
The Beloved is incapable of violating your soul.
His affection awaits unprompted trust,
His heart quivers with joy,
In the waiting to bestow on you eternal treasures…
But, so far,
You chase fantasy and wrathfully feed illusion.
And yet, the Beloved awaits.

Alma Eros
O cálice

A chuva benéfica e abundante cai dos céus
Mitigando a sede da terra.
Assim também, o Amado faz chover sobre os homens
Os poderes e as bênçãos.
No entanto, choras e desesperas...
Por que não recolheste a tempo a tua parte?
– Nada vi – responderás...
É porque teus olhos estavam nevoados na atmosfera do sonho.

O Senhor passa todos os dias,
Distribuindo os dons celestiais,
Mas as ânforas do teu coração vivem transbordando de
                               substâncias estranhas.

Aqui, guardas o vinagre dos desenganos,
Acolá, o envenenado licor dos caprichos.
O Amado é incapaz de violentar a tua alma.
Seu carinho aguarda a confiança espontânea,
Seu coração freme de júbilo,
Na expectativa de entregar-te os tesouros eternos...
Mas, até agora,
Persegues a fantasia e alimentas curiosamente a ilusão.
Todavia, o Amado espera.

And the day shall come,
On the long road of fate,
When you shall extend to his infinite love
The chalice of an empty, clean heart.

E dia virá,
Na estrada longa do destino,
Em que estenderás ao seu amor infinito
O cálice do coração lavado e vazio.

Marta
Never Isolate Yourself

Never isolate yourself between the springs of life;
Life is the eternal good that has been given us,
So that we would multiply it indefinitely…
And the soul that we leave,
To suffering or well-being,
Is a desert with no oasis,
Where other souls feel thirst and hunger.

To multiply life
Is to love without restriction
The flower, the bird, the hearts,
Everything that surrounds us.
To soften others' pains,
To smile to the miserable,
To bless the path that takes us
From the dark towards the light;
To thank God, merciful Father,
The firmament, the moonlight, the dawn,

To read your star-forged epic,
To have the naïve kindness of children,
To weave the eternal thread of hope
Through which one rises to Heaven;

Marta
Nunca te isoles

Nunca te isoles entre os mananciais da vida;
A vida é o eterno bem que nos foi dado,
Para que o multiplicássemos indefinidamente...
E a alma que se abandona,
Ao sofrimento ou ao bem-estar,
É um deserto sem oásis,
Onde outras almas sentem fome e sede.

Multiplicar a vida
É amar sem restrições
A flor, a ave, os corações,
Tudo o que nos rodeia.
Atenuar a dor alheia,
Sorrir aos infelizes,
Bendizer o caminho que nos leva
Da treva para luz;
Agradecer a Deus, que é Pai bondoso,
O firmamento, o luar, as alvoradas,

Ler a sua epopéia feita de astros,
Ter a bondade ingênua das crianças,
Tecer o fio eterno da esperança
Por onde se sobe ao Céu;

To smile, bring light, give affection,
To give everything we may muster,
It is all to love multiplying the life,
That extends endless in the Infinite.

To give a lesson in patience if we suffer,
To give a little bliss as we delight,
Is to keep the seed
Of Life
In fertile parcels,
And which will yield
Friendly shadows to rest,
Garments of scented flowers
And fruit, by the thousands,
To nourish our joys
In the starry gardens…

Dar sorrisos, dar luzes, dar carícias,
Dar tudo quanto temos,
Tudo isto é amar multiplicando a vida,
Que se estende infinita no Infinito.

Dar a lição de paciência se sofremos,
Dar um pouco de gozo se gozamos,
É guardarmos a semente
Da Vida
Em leivas verdejantes,
E a qual há de nos dar
Sombras amigas para descansarmos,
Indumentos de flores perfumosas
E frutos aos milhares,
Para nutrir as nossas alegrias
Nos jardins estelares…

Unknown
Meditating

I was one of those souls who lived
Without knowing the paradises of the Earth,
And those who only the bitterness of smiles
Through the night of pains, have they known.

Not that I was miserable and hapless,
For I was also human among humans,
And through my days, and years,
If I wanted pleasure, pleasure I would have.

It's that after feeling deep in the chest
Man's attitude in this life,
Heart deceived, soul deluded,
Secluded from the Pure and the Perfect,

My being which had dreamt of Humanity
As a stalk of scented flowers,
Saw souls shiver, hapless,
Under the weight of their own inequity.

Um Desconhecido
Meditando

Eu fui daquelas almas que viveram
Sem conhecer da Terra os paraísos,
Que somente a amargura dos sorrisos
Pela noite das dores conheceram.

Não que eu fosse infeliz e desditoso,
Pois fui também humano entre os humanos,
E através dos meus dias, dos meus anos,
Se eu quisesse gozar, teria o gozo.

É que ao sentir no âmago do peito
A atitude do homem nessa vida,
Coração enganado, alma iludida,
Afastado do Puro e do Perfeito,

O meu ser que sonhara a Humanidade
Qual um ramo de flores perfumosas,
Viu as almas tremerem, desditosas,
Sob o peso da própria iniqüidade.

And cut off in the great sufferings
Of being alone, on the roughness of the roads,
I found pleasure through thorns,
While trailing the tracks of torment.

For in the small world of my soul,
When misadventures covered me in pain,
I glimpsed the bright, pure light
That brought me peace, plenty, and calm:

– It was the light that came to me from the vision
Of seeing the Christ-Love, between exhaustion,
And rejoiced then, from seeing my own arms
Wrapped around the cross of trials.

E isolado nos grandes sofrimentos
De ser só, na aspereza dos caminhos,
Encontrei o prazer pelos espinhos,
Ao trilhar os carreiros dos tormentos.

Pois no mundo pequeno da minhalma,
Quando em dor me envolvia a desventura,
Eu vislumbrava a luz brilhante e pura
Que me trazia a paz, bonança e calma:

– Era a luz que me vinha da visão
De ver o Cristo-Amor, entre cansaços,
E tinha então prazer de ver meus braços
Enlaçados na cruz da provação.

jeremy fernando ·
on afterwords;
or, what comes after the word…

|

Often real understanding and true love come to us hidden under the cloak of anonymity.
                    – Emmanuel in Xavier, *Nosso Lar*, 11

A writing from elsewhere, from another. A writing that acknowledges that it comes from somewhere other than the hand of the author, from another author as it were. A writing that foregrounds what Hélène Cixous never lets us forget; that "we have been caught up in citation ever since we said the first words mama or papa."[1]

But what does it mean to inhabit another's voice? Or, perhaps the more appropriate question is: what does it mean to allow another to inhabit oneself? Can we really tell the difference, separate the voice of Chico Xavier from any other, all others? This would also be the question of calls, of callings: does Chico answer the call of another, or is the call his only because he has answered it. And as one is attempting to write in response, write towards a response, write as a response, the question that continually haunts the writing is: *is one really responding to a call?* Or, more precisely, *is one responding to a call or is the call always already a reading, an interpretive gesture, a version of the response?* In attempting to respond to a call, are we also already writing that call into being?

Here, we should try not to forget that as we are being inhabited, the very thing (if it can be called that) that comes into us might well turn into, become, a habit. And this is the very realm where forgetting inscribes itself into memory: for, something is habitual only when it is so much a part of us that we no longer have to think of it, are no longer conscious of it, when we no longer even remember that we are doing it. It is an act that we have forgotten, that is part of us only because we have forgotten it. This might well be the danger that Plato alludes to when he warns us of the power of art. After all, the moment when craft (*tekhnē*) opens itself to art – to the whisper of the *daimōn* – is the point when the artisan is so immersed in her craft that (s)he becomes, is, the medium for the possibility of art; this is the moment where (s)he forgets herself in, and through, her craft; when (s)he inhabits her craft, where her craft inhabits her. And this is also the point when (s)he opens herself to the unknown, to the unknowable; where her very being itself might be ruptured by this opening.

In, and through, these thoughts, these questions, it is not too difficult to hear echoes of Saint Augustine, who opens his text – *Confessions* – with a series of questions: "how can one call for what one does not recognise? Without such recognition, one could be calling for something else, Or is calling for you the way to recognise you?"[2] Is one called, or does one have to answer a call? Or, more pertinently, *is there even a call if it is not answered?*; which is a question of, *is the status of a call dependent on a response?* Augustine's reflections might well have been a remix of the well-known episode in *Genesis* where Yahweh calls for Abraham, calls out Abraham's name.[3] The fact that Yahweh has to call twice (or even thrice depending on the version you are reading) suggests that Abraham ignores this call at least once. Which is completely understandable: divine calls are very rarely pleasant. He turned out to be completely on the mark here – in answering the call, he had to, or at least was called to, murder his son. The fact that Isaac was replaced at the last minute by a ram makes no difference to the fact that Abraham was called to commit filicide.[4] Hence, we should never forget the potential danger that answering a call entails. This is, of course, not lost on the writers of scripture as the story of the Nazarene ends with another famous call – this time, a call for help. Nearing death, Jesus of Nazareth looks up to the skies and utters, *Eloi Eloi lama sabachthani*[5] which is usually translated as *My God, my god, why have you forsaken me?* An unanswered call, put on call-waiting as it were, a call that also echoes helplessness, desperation; a cry of *daddy, daddy, where the fuck are you?* Answering a call can lead to death; not-having your call answered, not answering a call, might just be as fatal.

But perhaps, what disturbs us most is the fact that Chico refuses to put the phone down. For, we should never forget that in *Poetry from Beyond the Grave,* all the poems are signed off with the names of others, are named as poems of others. Where Chico is the scribe, inscribing the sounds of others: taking dictation, as it were. Which is not to say – as Avital Ronell shows us in *Dictations*[6] – that the secretary isn't as much the writer as the one dictating, that the scribe isn't inscribing as well; that (s)he doesn't leave her mark, that Chico doesn't leave his hand, on the text. But, this is a stamp that isn't the mark of an author, that doesn't claim any authority – for, it is a writing that responds to, foregrounds, the voice of another, that maintains the relationality with the other. And by not doing so, Chico turns away from the very gesture of authorship – the *caesura*. For, in order to become an author, for authorship to occur, one has to – at least momentarily – cut from citationality, quotation, stake a claim on a work, put one's own stamp – name – on it. Move from being a scribe, taking notes, being dictated to, to the one who inscribes, makes her mark, marks as her own, brands it – authors. And as we ponder upon the certitude, certainty, needed to transform oneself into an author, the author, we might also consider how – along with it – echoes of calls to *grow up, stand on your own feet, make your voice heard,* are resounding here.

So perhaps, what disturbs us most when we encounter Chico Xavier is his insistence on writing like a child. Continually copying. Refusing to make his own mark – or, more accurately, refusing to take credit, take sole credit, for the mark he is making. Taking down notes from the other. Indulging in citationality. Foregrounding the fact that *these are the words of mama or papa*. Refusing to grow up, as it were.

Turning Babel into a gift.[7]

And perhaps, what causes us the most anxiety is precisely his foregrounding of the child. As Avital Ronell reminds us, "childhood cannot be restricted to a historical phase in human development – it returns every time one is tortured by nonrepresentable feelings or one is stalled, stuttering, stuck in a place without recourse or comprehension."[8] But, as one is stammering, one should not forget that these uncertain utterances, small whispers even, open little ruptures, tears, sometimes even tears, moments when we well up; possibilities. After all, writing is a form of, from, scratching (*scribere*); and as Nietzsche teaches us, each writing (*schreiben*) always already brings with it a potential scream (*schreien*). The scream, screech, of a child – pure language, where there is little to no signification, but full of significance, possibility, pure potentiality. Perhaps that is the true stigma; the mark that comes from elsewhere, from beyond, a mark that marks – and all we can ever know is that it marks.

And even worse, marks us as children, as a child. As one that has no authority. For, if a child, one is not father, one is not the source, origin (*auctor*).

Which brings us to the paradox of authority: to have authority one has to be acknowledged by another, as an – the – authority. For, authority cannot be granted to oneself – there has to be another. Someone else has to deem one an authority on something; and, more than that, willingly. Otherwise, it would merely be an imposition of the self upon another, one will over another: that would be a situation of power, terror even, but certainly not authority. And since authority has to be granted, this suggests that it always already comes from elsewhere. Which also suggests that relationality is the very condition of authority. However, the very moment authority is granted to another, (s)he becomes an absolute other, unquestionable, unknowable. Daddy – to whom one can no longer speak with; where one is only spoken to. And thus, the very relationality that opens the possibility of authority – a relationality that is granted – is ruptured, shattered, by this act of authorisation. Where the moment you grant it to daddy, perhaps all you can ever say is, *where the fuck are you…*

And if reading is of the order of the question, a quest to respond to and with, the moment one cedes authority to the author of the text – the point at which one deems a writer to be the origin, creator, father, of the text – not only is the author beyond one's capacity, the text itself become unreadable.

The trouble is: at the end of writing – at the point where one wants the writing to be sent out into the world – one has to name oneself as author; write, put, one's name down. And at the very moment of doing so, one also undoes one's authority – for, authority must be given to one. Why another gives it to one, why it is given to another, is another question entirely; one that perhaps has no answer. To compound matters, the moment one is authorised – perhaps through publishers, through a press, through a legal system that deems one the rightful author of a text – one is no longer able to read the text; one is separated from it. The text is emancipated from its author. Outside (*ex-*) the grip of the ownership (*mancipium*); away from the grip (*manus*; hand) of the one who owns, the one who takes (*capere*) control over one. But once outside the law, one might well also be beyond the pale: for, one must never forget that if one is in language – at least in a manner that can be understood, even if the understanding is provisional, momentary – one is always before the law. But once put before said law, language, and by extension, the text, is also no longer one's own: it, and one – and one's relationality with the text, the law – is always already preceded by norms, mores, boundaries. Perhaps then, the only way to slip past the law, go by the gatekeeper, is to remain nameless: after all, the law can only be enacted on one it can name, call before itself.

Which might be why Chico Xavier – in attempting to open himself to the voices of others, attempting to respond to the other poets, attempting to open the text to voices of other poets – has to first deny, refuse, paternity over the text.[9] But, it is not a refusal that entails a wounding, a complete closing off. For, even as Chico foregrounds the voice of the other, even as he refuses a claim over another, it is a turning away that does not fully turn its back; the relationality to the other is maintained. Perhaps then not a complete refusal; just that at the moment of saying, he utters – echoing another great voice from literature – "I prefer not to."[10]

And here, we should not forget that Bartleby escapes the curse of a first name, a given name; or at least we never get to know it. From all accounts, neither does the narrator, nor anyone else. Not only that, no one knows from whence he came. And it is only in this manner that Bartleby can perform his act of passive resistance: turning away every request, not by refusing engagement, but by engaging so he doesn't have to do so. For, even as he carries a family name – a familial affiliation, where he is in a line, perhaps even purchased (*mancipium*) already – by escaping the fact of a first name, he disappears within the lines of numerous possible Mr Bartlebys; he remains outside the possibility of certain identification, absolute signification. And perhaps this is also why, even as he foregrounds the otherness of the poems, the works, Chico Xavier also signs off on them: the collection *Poetry from Beyond the Grave* is in his name. For, without that gesture there would not be an acknowledgement of responsibility that it is he – and no other – that is responding to the call. However, in foregrounding the other(s), Chico is also positing himself as nothing other than a medium through which this call is answered.

As a telephone.

Or, as Clarice Lispector might say, "out of honest respect for true authorship, I quote the world, I quoted it, since it was neither me nor mine."[11]

By naming himself as the medium through which the others write – by naming himself the scrivener – Chico Xavier takes responsibility for what is not his, for what is not.

Quite unlike say Martin Heidegger, who refuses responsibility for responding to the call from the *Sturmabteilung*; dismissing his role, saying: "someone from the top command of the Storm Trooper University Bureau, SA section leader Baumann called me up. He demanded …"[12] Not a: I picked up the phone, answered the call. But a: it wasn't my choice, not even of my doing – after all "he demanded." Which translates to: how could I not do so, how could I even say no. Which is also an attempt at transposing genres: it is not so much a call but a summons: this was no ordinary sound made from a distance – he was a Storm Trooper, a figure from, and of, authority; it was daddy calling me… A strange response, particularly since it was coming from someone who had devoted his thinking to events, to possibilities, to the call of otherness. Why did some calls matter, and why did others not: and is it ever possible to dismiss a call that one has answered? Is it ever possible to constitute it as a call – or even a summons – if it was not first answered? But, as Avital Ronell reminds us in *The Telephone*

Book, "if Heidegger was there to receive the SA call, it is because he first had to accept the *Be-ruf,* or position, from which that ordering call could be picked up, that of rector, a position he held from 1933 to 1934." Thus, this call "takes place within a context of a prior call, though not in terms of a subject's desire but in those of an inescapable calling or vocation."[13] If Heidegger could not turn down daddy's call, it was because he had first accepted the call, the *ruf,* to be a son. For, the very condition of its possibility as a call is that one answers, even if that answer is to turn away, to reject, to refuse the content of the call; the call itself is always already answered at the very moment one recognises that it is a call. And more precisely – since one can never know if the call was even intended for one – by recognising its status as a call, one has already adopted it for oneself; and by doing so, opened oneself to its effects, to being affected by the call; by doing so, it is authorised as a call.

Perhaps then, we might consider the gesture of Chico Xavier to be one of acknowledging, foregrounding even, that it is he – Chico Xavier and no other – that is picking up these calls, but that the content of these calls, the poems, are not his. That he is the one that is writing the call, inscribing – transcribing – the writing that comes to him from elsewhere; that he hears, that he is attending to, a call that he hears within, a call that is not just of the ear – after all, there is no mention of a sound that is heard by any others around him – but a sound written into his mind, even as he is writing the sound.

Psycho graphein.

Writing of the mind. Writing on the mind. Writing that is of the mind. One in which it is impossible to differentiate whether what is written, what we can see to be written, is what is written in the first place. Leaving aside whether the one who is writing, the one whom is being written on, can know, with any measure of certainty – and here we should take measure, and our inability to measure, extremely seriously, as we are no longer in the realm of the ratio, of reason – whether what (s)he, in this case Chico, is reading is what is being written, the question that is opened is that of translation: of the movement between *psycho* and *graphein*. Which is also what happens to the movement, transference, journey, between reading and writing – keeping in mind that journey opens the register of the quest that remains throughout this question.

A *séance*: one in which one cannot quite differentiate the dancer from the dance, the writer from the one reading, the reading of the written from what is inscribed. Not just between the one who writes and the voices (s)he is attending to, but also between her reading and her writing, between her and herself.

Where perhaps all that can be said is that (s)he is attempting to report what (s)he has heard, what (s)he hears in her head.

And if Chico is responding to, reporting, the voice of the other, this is the condition *par excellence* of testimony; keeping in mind Jacques Derrida's reminder that fiction is the very condition, groundless ground, *Abgrund,* of testimony; that it is hinged paradoxically on the fact that the one witnessing has to have been there, that (s)he is witnessing to what only (s)he could have seen, and yet, at the same time, (s)he has to be witnessing to a universality, to what anyone else in her place would have seen. Moreover, one can only testify to something that has happened, something in the past: which suggests that it is always already a construction, narrated, reconstructed – an act of memory. Bringing with it all the problems of forgetting: for, if one can never control forgetting, if one can never know what one has forgotten, it might always already be inscribed, written into, memory, remembering.

Which might be why Chico Xavier has to poetically testify. For, as Derrida continues, "the testimonial act is poetic or it is not, from the moment it must invent its language and form itself in an incommensurable performative."[14] An imaginative moment, one of creation: for, the one who testifies must first choose, select, write their moment – inscribe their version of time itself. Here, one might also tune in to, channel, Giorgio Agamben's reminder that "the poet – the contemporary – must firmly hold his gaze on his own time." He continues: "but what does he who sees his time actually see? What is this demented grin on the face of his century?... The contemporary is he who firmly holds his gaze on his own time so as to perceive not its light but rather its darkness. All eras, for those who experience contemporariness, are obscure. The contemporary is precisely the person who knows how to see this obscurity, who is able to write by dipping his pen in the obscurity of the present."[15] The one who testifies is the one is also aware that her testimony is fraught with the unknown, the unknowability of what (s)he testifies. Which suggests that the act of testimony is an act of authoring which bears all risks of possible shiftings, adjustments, augmentations: in other words, always already with the potential of a slant – bias. Keeping in mind that a bias is a part of, a fragment: not just in relation with a fragmented whole, but also as a whole that is a fragment. Not forgetting that as we read, we can only read a part of, in parts, that all reading itself is always already a fragment. For, all we can do is attend to a part of a text, a fragment apart from the text as such – but in that moment of attention, the part is also our whole, occupies our entire being. Perhaps as we read, the readings form a sequence – one of a group of other readings; but also, a singular entity onto itself. However, any sequence is held together by the *zero*, a non-number, the *cipher*, the *secret*.

Perhaps, the exact relationship between the fragment and what it is also a part of, the part and the whole, always remains beyond us, before us, dark to us. So, even as Chico Xavier tells us in *Nosso Lar* that "the spirit body presents within it a complete history of the actions practiced on Earth,"[16] we should keep in mind that this is a spirit body as the site of testimony – a site to be read by others, a site of reading. But even as we read, even as Chico Xavier reads and writes, even as we read the writings of Chico Xavier, this movement, this quest, this translation, this attempt to respond with a text in a moment of time, in the contemporaneous, is always also a moment shrouded in darkness. In other words, reading is an act of faith. And here, one must never forget that those who testified to their faith were always considered mad. Or, worse: burnt at the stake.

Thus, staking this particular claim as a response to the other, writing – authoring whilst acknowledging that what is written is from another, that the authority of the writing is from beyond – is a pure gift; beyond calculation, calculability, accountability, valuation, even reason; but always only an attempt to respond with, reach out to, another; or a curse. Not that they are ever quite separate from each other.

And here, we might finally be able to take Marshall McLuhan's claim "the medium is the message"[17] – or, even better, the error that eventually became a title: "the medium is the massage"[18] – seriously. For, it is not just the message in the sense of the content, but more importantly, the medium shapes what we take to be the content itself. That the author – Chico Xavier – is the one who massages the messages from elsewhere, not to fit a particular pre-determined box, code, intent, but more profoundly that the shaping, framing, occurs the moment the message passes through him: that he is its – the – very frame. And here, it is not too difficult to hear another lesson from Tamar Guimarães: that "if history is the impossible conversation with the dead, as Michel de Certeau suggested, then the medium has a privileged role as a history writer."[19] The fact that Guimarães is echoing the thought, the voice, of Certeau, of another, here – mediating Certeau, being his medium – should not be lost on us. Thus, as we attempt to read *Poetry from Beyond the Grave*, we might bear in mind that we are also reading Chico Xavier, even as he remains in the background, in the dark: that he is the home to the messages even as they might well remain unhomely in, and through, him: he is their haunt, even as they haunt him, haunt us through him. Remember that this reading of Chico as a frame is also always a reading of him with his text, a reading of his text with him – a relation. So, even as he might be the home, it is also – without possibility of referentiality – our home.

Nosso Lar.

Thus, a relationality premised on the possibility of relationality, a relationality before relationality itself. Not just in the darkness that remains in Chico Xavier's response to the poet-ghosts, ghostly poetry, but in our attempts to read *Poetry from Beyond the Grave*.

A leap of faith that we might – one might – even be able to do so.

II

What of the name of the writer?

Not of the text; not of the one who writes the text; but the one who writes on the text – who writes as the reader, who leaves a mark of having read, of having attempted to read. Who attempts to write as a reader. Or, perhaps more accurately: who writes in the voice of the one who reads.

Prosopopoeia. Even if this mimicry is of one's own voice.[20]

Fernando – the name of the one who writes, the one who attempts to respond.

And here, if one wanted, one could even claim that the Portuguese origin of the name gives it a certain authority – particularly in relation with a Brazilian poet. A claim of, and through, language; a claim of a shared language or, at least, a notion of a shared heritage – no matter how problematic that might be culturally, geographically, and in this case spiritually even. This would be an appeal to a complicity of histories, of shared stories – even as much as there might well be no commonality to begin with. Almost a case of buying shares into the tale in order to feel a part of it: an economic kind of claim – an attempt to simulate a common *oikos*.

But, we must also not forget that, in this instance, Fernando has been shifted from a first – a given name – to a last, the *sur-*, the excessive name: the name that continues to haunt all generations of those that bear the mark of it. So, even as this particular Fernando is unable to respond directly to the call of Chico Xavier, it might well come through the name, his name, my name; a name that is both mine and that always already precedes me.

The ghostly name.

Completely appropriate considering how Hamlet's reaction to his father's revelation, his plea to "remember me" is to turn scribe: "*he writes*: So, uncle, there you are. Now to my word: it is 'Adieu, adieu, remember me'. I have sworn't."[21] It is inscribed: both the farewell, and the reminder to remember – perhaps a farewell to remembering. For, we should never forget that the ghost remains nameless. But, even as the ghost remains nameless, its spectre remains the centre of, central to, the tale. Perhaps, one might even posit that it is only because the ghost is heard by Hamlet and no one else that the spectre can dominate the proceedings: if there was anyone else to verify the apparition's accusations, it would be fairly certain, fairly easy to ascertain, that Claudius was guilty; its aural absence from everyone else maintains the possibility that it is only a voice in Hamlet's head. And here, one should keep in mind Plato's warning that writing is always only a trace of absence – a means of reminding oneself rather than memory itself. Thus, picking up a pencil and scribbling down the ghost's message is a response to the absent – and hence, the perfect response; perhaps, the only possible response. Particularly if what is written is a vow, a promise; thus, an inscription with no referentiality – which suggests that writing also opens the possibility of an infinite delay, a remembering that is only to come.

Writing: an inscription in order to remind one of what one might otherwise have forgotten. An inscription in order to allow one to forget. However, one should not forget that one has no control over whether – and what – one forgets. Perhaps then, writing opens the possibility that the memory can leave one's *habitus*. In order to open the possibility of absence itself: which is tautological – for, it is only a possibility if it is still absent; even if one maintains that a possibility is to come, it has to be unknowable until it arrives.

Possibility. Absence. Both of the order of spectres. Ghosts.

Which suggests that, at best, we might only be able to catch a glimpse – perhaps a whisper; depending on the manner in which the spectre allows itself to be heard, seen, experienced – of it. And if only a glimmer, it might always only be a part of it; a fragment – either a tiny element that we see, or a tiny element that remains; not that the two are antonymous. For, either way, one can never know as the part that remains, that we see, is always beyond our knowledge, our knowing, is always apart from us.

A reading that can only be speculative; for, it is can only attend to specks.

Reading through the small. *Pequeno*. Perhaps we might even call it a gesture *toward a minor reading*. Keeping in mind that a minor reading, like a minor literature, "doesn't come from a minor language; it is rather that which as minority constructs within a major language."[22] Thus, a reading of language that is the same language, but always already open to possibilities – perhaps even possibilities not quite known within the language itself. A reading that "makes [language] vibrate with a new intensity. [That] oppose[s] a purely intensive usage of language to all symbolic or even significant or simply signifying usages of it."²³ And what exemplifies that intensity more than the language of children, utterances that are within language – otherwise one would not even be able to recognise them as utterances – but are not even versions, variations, of regular, prescribed, usage but instead are wholly new introductions into language itself: not in the sense of meaning – far from it – but to the senses themselves, where the utterance is a pure utterance; escaping all possibility of signification, or even significance. And as Gilles Deleuze and Félix Guattari point out, it is "children [who] are well skilled in the exercise of repeating a word, the sense of which is only vaguely felt, in order to make it vibrate around itself."²⁴ Where language itself is a playground for exploration, for play: where all one can say is that language itself becomes curious, open, a possibility: a "language torn from sense, conquering sense, bringing about an active neutralization of sense, [where it] no longer finds its value in anything but an accenting of the word, an inflection."²⁵

A minor reading; or, a reading of minors.

But here, we might also try not to forget Avital Ronell's warning that "the child constitutes a security risk for the house of philosophy. It crawls in, setting off a lot of noise."²⁶ Much like how, "the poet, irremediably split between exaltation and vulgarity, between the autonomy that produces the concept within intuition and the foolish earthly being, functions as a contaminant for philosophy – a being who at least since Plato, has been trying to read and master an eviction notice served by philosophy. The poet as genius continues to threaten and fascinate, menacing the philosopher with the beyond of knowledge. Philosophy cringes."[27]

The child as poet; the poet as child – the son through the little one – *o chico através do pequeno*.

After all, we might recall that the child, the infant, is the one before language; the one who is open to the possibility of language itself. The one who is open to the whisper(s) of language. Here, a question opens: considering the notion that the philosopher is the lover of wisdom – remembering that wisdom comes through a whisper from the *daimōn* – we might begin to ask ourselves why one lover is warning against another? If the philosopher is in love with wisdom, then is the poet perhaps his rival, his challenger, for that very love? And here, one must remember that Plato – through Socrates – openly declares that Homer is his favourite. Moreover, by adopting both his own voice, whilst mixing it with Socrates', Plato is adopting the form of poetry that he warns most about – *prosopopoeia*. Thus, the warning almost serves more as a homage to poetry than anything else.

Much like how telling a child not to open the door only ensures that is precisely what (s)he would do. Not that the warning to the child is aimed at eliciting the opposite response: if that were true, there would not be a punishment. But, more radically, that each prohibition – opening our registers to the teachings of St. Paul here – already brings with it its subversion. However, even as we say that, it requires an act of reading; and at the moment the child reads, even if (s)he is reading to subvert the law, (s)he has opened herself to language – at that point, (s)he is no longer outside of language. (S)he is now brought before language itself, before the law. Recalling that each act of resisting requires an engagement, resistance, thus, always already opens one to precisely what one is attempting to subvert. This is the true seductive power of the law: by opening itself to being challenged, it ensnares one. To enact the confrontation, one has to stand before the law; and at that very moment the law itself comes into being – what comes before the law, its pre-condition as it were, is the fact that there has to be someone standing before it. Thus, it is the challenge – the subversion itself – that calls the law into being.

One must also remember that the source of all learning – and all teaching – lies in mimesis, in repetition, in habit. Once the *habitus* is opened to the possibility of invasion, of intervention, of otherness, there is quite possibly no way of distinguishing whether the mimesis is that of reproduction, or if there is always already a productive aspect to it. And this is one of the main reasons Plato – through Socrates – ejects a particular kind of poet; on the grounds of effecting effeminacy on the populace – for, good poetry moves you, affects you, transports you, shifts you beyond reason, puts you out of your mind. However, Plato also teaches us that rhetoric in its highest form requires divine inspiration by way of the *daimōn*, or the muse. This moment of divine intervention is one that seizes you – perhaps even causes you to cease – takes you beyond yourself. In other words, a good rhetorician must always already be open to the possibility of otherness – the same otherness that possibly resides in the feminine. One could also trace this to the poet that he loved, and feared, most – Homer. Perhaps the effect of effeminacy that Homer's poetry opens is precisely the source of its power: through listening to Homer, one's body, one's *habitus* is opened to the possibility of the feminine. Moreover, if learning cannot be controlled, the very notion of teaching itself is shifted from a master-student relationality to one where the master is potentially changed as well; and this is crucial as Plato's teachings are ultimately about the education of a good person – where the soul is at stake. The relationality between the master and the student is not only inter-changing, but one in which the one who is teaching and the one learning, might not be differentiable at any point. All that can be said is that they are in a relationality; which means that one is ultimately unable to locate the locus of knowledge, of wisdom – the site of which Plato is attempting to convince us is the sole domain of the philosopher. At the moment the muse whispers into one's ear, one ceases to be, and becomes a medium for poetry – and since this possession is beyond one's cognitive knowledge, this is also a moment of divine wisdom. In other words, there is no difference between poetry and wisdom – the moment of poetry is the moment of wisdom. And this might be the very reason for the philosopher's aversion to poets. Not so much because they may corrupt the youth (this is, after all, the aim of all thinking, all philosophy), but precisely because in order to do so, the philosopher must wait for a moment of possession, for divine musing, for poetry.

Thus, all thought, all thinking, all philosophy, is nothing but the waiting for the possibility of poetry itself.

And more than that: if the moment of wisdom is one that comes to one as it potentially continually also eludes one, it is always also a moment that is before language. Thus, at the moment one is opened to the possibility of wisdom, poetry, one is always also a child. Small. Pequeno.

Where, for a moment, all one can do – perhaps all one should do – is to roll with it, flow with it. And all one can say is: "for a minute there I lost myself, I lost myself."[28] Which might sound like a too easy, too convenient, way of slipping past responsibility – an excuse for not being held accountable for one's actions. However, one must not forget that one can only be affected when one opens oneself to the possibility in the first place. For, even as "myself", my self, is lost, one should not ignore the echoes of the fact that it is the "I" who loses it. Even if one maintains that the "I" is ever changing, constantly in flux, at any particular moment, there is an "I" to a response, an "I" that chooses to pick up the call in the first place. And one must never forget that to answer the call one must be in language – to do so, one must first stand before it.

So, even as I might posit, foreground, the fact that my reading of Chico Xavier is a small one, one mediated through the small, through Pequeno, at the back of my mind, I am still haunted by the possibility of an accusation from beyond the grave: where he thunders, "Treacherous Fernando! You'll now, this instant, pay for the wrong you've did to me! With my hands I'll tear out that wicked heart of yours that is filled with every crime, especially with fraud and trickery!"[29]

III

...interpretation – promise – séance...

> *Whenever there is a promise, something other than the promise and something other than language – or simply another language – is also spoken. What is promised is always something other than understanding, other than another understanding, and other than an alteration of understanding alone. Something unpromisable.*
> – Hamacher, *Premises*, 142

For, in order to promise, there has to be something that is only to come, something not quite yet, something beyond; where the something that is promised cannot even have the status of a thing, or at least a known thing – therefore, there can never be a referent to the promise. Which means that it is an utterance – since the promise has to be uttered, otherwise it cannot yet be a promise – without any correspondence: *catachresis*. Completely illegitimate; an utterance that not only cannot be verified, but might never be verifiable. But, at the same time, might well have occurred without one ever even knowing – a coming to be outside of, exterior to, what is uttered. For, one should never forget that "interpretation is never the interpretation of a given other – whether it be a text, a person, a fact, an event, or a history – but it is always the laying out of what lays itself out in view of something else entirely."[30] Where the "unpromisable" cannot be promised precisely because it is not, is not quite yet, cannot be, stated.

At this point, it might be appropriate to momentarily consider the title of Werner Hamacher's text, his collection of essays, his appropriation (even as I am seizing onto his text, his words, his thought; promising – without ever explicitly stating it – that I am fairly, faithfully, attending to his thinking) of assailings on particular notions, topics: *Premises*.

And more specifically, *what is a premise?*

Which is a tricky question: considering the very form of it is in itself a premise. For, without the proposition that is set (*premissa, propositio*) one cannot even begin to address, let alone have an object of, to, address. Thus, the ability to address itself – to have an address to send one's thought towards, as it were – is itself a premise. And here, one should not forget that one often calls one's home, one's premises. Which opens the register of the *oikos*, bringing with it notions of calculation, measurement, rationality, reason, ratio. For, in order to meaningfully think about anything, there have to be limits, boundaries – something has to be excluded, out of bounds, too much, beyond the pale. Here, it is not too difficult to hear echoes of the *præ* (before) in "pre-", where one is made to stand before. And here, let us momentarily note the dossier of rules, laws, regulations, that one is standing before – after all, even as what is promised in the premise might be the "unpromisable," the yet to be promised, the unknowable promise, it is not as if we will admit everything as a promise, it is not as if just anything is admissible. One should also not forget that the second half of the word, "mise" is about sending, sending off (*mittere*) – thus always already out of bounds, external, out of the home. Thus, a threshold, but always also more than that – a missive, missile even, that is away, going from, but carrying echoes, messages, from home. So, as we are hearing calls from another, as we are attempting to respond to calls from beyond, we should bear in mind that our responses not only open ourselves – our self – to the possibility of another, but are also a launching of ourselves through the call, at the call we think calls us. This is a response in the threshold, the in-between, as Lucretius envisages it – in the skin between, the *simulacra*. And at this point, this moment of coming together, there is a distant communication, *tele-communicado,* that is away, apart, from the two in communion; even if the two are very much a part of it.

A communicating that is always also *ex-communicado*. Where my premises are not mine as yours are not yours, where my premise and yours are also neither mine nor yours; a shared premise –

mi casa es su casa; nosso lar.

Perhaps here, we should slow down momentarily, and linger on the *es,* the *is*. And recall that even as one is attempting to attend to the text, to the call of the text, to the possibilities that are of, and from, the text, there is – however provisionally – a moment where one responds to a single aspect of it, a moment when one says something of the text. Which is the moment when one says *something is like something else*; the moment when one attends to the possibility of opening what is read to the potential of another; the moment when two readings come together. This is the moment of interpretation; keeping in mind the registers of among, between, *inter-*, that come with it.

Thus, the moment of interpretation is not just one that entails a judgment, a call, on something, but one that also involves a relationality with the very thing that one is judging. Thus, as one is making that call, one is also being called. Which suggests that even as one may think one is interpreting, the one interpreting is always already being interpreted – a being in interpretation only because of the possibility of interpretation. And thus, "if the one who activates interpretation is 'unhinged', so too is the interpretation as act. Interpretation is not a performative; it is not an act in the sense of a praxis performed by a subject, nor is it the deed of an empirical or transcendental doer, whether this doer is called will, grammar, or faith. Rather, interpretation is the aporetic – the self-missing – premise of every possible performance, a pre- and mis-performation. It has no Being, is not a transhistorical substance but a becoming without ground or goal, at the limit of 'itself', neither act nor fact, but – with all the unresolved tension this concept connotes – an affect. Interpretation is, in short, the word for the aporia of interpretation: for the experience of a nonsubjective process turning into a subject. And the experience is itself an aporetic one – hence an affect – because only at the point where a subject is not yet and will never be is it possible to undergo the experience of a still outstanding experience, the experience of an impossible experience and thus the experience of the impossibility of the aporia of experience."[31] In other words, interpretation is nothing more, and infinitely nothing less, than the promise of the possibility of interpretation. Keeping in mind that "promising means nothing else – a promise of the mere possibility of making promises."[32] Which is not to say that the one that is promising is not responsible for the promise, for the utterance of the promise; for, even as it is perhaps always only in potentiality, it must also be uttered. A promise only exists – if it can be said to exist, to be; but at least it is always in becoming – in and through language. But here, we must never forget that "speaking a language means nothing else than speaking as one who does not yet have a language."[33]

This suggests that the very promise – the site, premise, and the condition for the possibility of interpretation, and of reading – is that of language itself.

The moment we constitute – or attempt to think of – language as a site, we open the dossier of language as a space, or even – to echo an earlier register – of language as a home. One that, since we are still tuning into the scale, rhythms, of the promise, is both accommodating and yet remains unfamiliar to us. Thus, even as interpretation is hinged around the possibilities of language, any attempt to approach language is itself always already an attempt at interpretation. Which suggests that there might never be an end, or at least an endpoint that can be known, to interpretation. As Hamacher continues, "the possibility of infinite interpretations makes every particular interpretation and therefore the very concept of interpretation contingent. The possibility that the world, the perspective of the will, and interpretation could always be another one and, a limine, none at all – this potential of other possibilities that interpretation can never exhaust – inscribes an uncontrollable alterity into the very concept of interpretation and forbids, strictly speaking, all talk of interpretation itself. Tinged by other interpretations and non-interpretations, every interpretation must also be capable of being something other than interpretation and, *a limine,* no interpretation at all. Every interpretation is exposed to its other and to its Not: each one from the beginning an ex-posed, interrupted interpretation."[34]

In interpretation, in language, in thinking as such, we are always on a *limen,* threshold – an unhomely home. In haunts that are exposed to hauntings.

But just because we can never know if an interpretation is correct, true, or even an interpretation at all, does not mean that anything goes – this is not quite *vale tudo.* Far from it. For, even as it "cannot construct a theory of truth as correspondence [it] must set out the conditions of possibility of, the genesis of, and the imperative demand for such a truth… Interpretation, being interpretative, is not a constative statement but the performance of truth, the truth itself as performance. But because the performance of the truth of interpretation – of this interpretation, which posits itself as truth and, positing itself as truth, performatively comes true – occurs in the precarious form of the imperative, and thus in the very form of an unfulfilled command; because it is, accordingly, not a perlocutionary but an illocutionary speech act; and because the language it commands has not yet come into being, the imperative occurs as a *pre-*locutionary 'speech act.'"[35] And since it resides in the pre- it is not only without object, it is also – since the interpreter can only be one in relation with the object of interpretation – without, before, subject. An "imperative," a call as law, that is both objectless and addressing no subject, that becomes an address, a call, an imperative, only when the subject responds to it, even though it might well not have ever been for her. Thus, the interpretive act lies in the very interpretation that the call is hers; an interpretation that comes before interpretation itself, is before the imperative that is interpretation; the interpretation that brings forth interpretation.

And since it is an interpretation before the possibility of interpretation, one can never quite say what it is, let alone whom is interpreting. Or perhaps, as Saint Augustine might confess: " – and here reason, for one flicker of an eye, reached the Is."[36] Where any utterance, any attempt to posit, to respond with, what is interpretation is in itself a leap of faith.

So, perhaps, very much *vale tudo*.

*

Which brings us back all the way to the beginning, to where I began, and the question of *where is this coming from?*; the question of the journey, the quest, the movement from elsewhere to the ear – momentarily leaving aside the possibility that there are potentially other receptors to calls – of Chico Xavier. For, one should remember that in responding to the calls from the other poems, the other poets, it is Chico that is granting a certain authorship to them: for, one must not forget that even though it is Chico's name that is on the front of the collection, covering the gathering of poems as it were, he names the poet from whom each poem comes from. And in doing so, he names it a poem; and the one named is named as poet.

Almost an echo of the whisper of the *daimōn*; except in this case, the one who receives, hears, the whispers responds with an inscription on the name of the whisperer. A response to the call, a reading of the call as call, with writing – perhaps a recognition that writing and reading cannot be divorced: if reading and interpretation (even interpretation as interpretation) are intertwined, any moment of reading that stakes a claim – that reads as it were – always involves a positing, taking a position, an inscribing, a writing, no matter how momentary; and the only way to know that there is writing, that one has written, is by reading. Hence, one cannot separate Chico Xavier's inscription of the work, the poems, from his interpretation of the work as poems, from his reading of them as works.

Thus, reading, interpretation, and authoring, authority, are housed in the same home, are always haunting each other. For, authority requires authorship from another, from elsewhere – it is sustained by another's reading, interpretation, of one as an author, as one with authority. It is a contract between one and another. Which means that in order for the notion of authorship, authoring, to stabilise itself – no matter how momentary this stasis is – all parties involved have to be standing before a law; or, at least, an idea, notion, of the law. So, even as the one who is author might well be sovereign, (s)he is a sovereign that cannot ground her own sovereignty. And more than that, if one's authority is only granted by another – but on the condition that it is granted before the law, a law that stands before not only the one being authored, but also the one granting the authority – this suggests that both are blind to the law itself: even as they are before it, it is external to them, beyond them. Hence, the source, as it were, of one's sovereignty remains veiled from her; (s)he is blind to how, and by whom, (s)he is authored. (S)he blind to her own origins, *auctor*, father. So, even as one is named author, the question that continues to haunt her is *who's your daddy?*

But even as we might consider reading, interpretation, writing, as a contractual situation, this does not mean that it is sterile, safe, certain. For, we must not forget that, in a contract one and another are intertwined, bringing with it is own risks; spillage, seepages, infections. One should never forget that one could contract syphilis from another. And since the condition of the law is that one is in a contract with said law – even if one was born into the law, thrown before the law, even if one never quite signed the contract – and the condition of the contract is the existence of the law, this suggests that the exact relationality between the law and its enactment, the notion of the law and its manifestation, in and through the contract, remains hidden from us, maintains itself as a potentially indecipherable secret. Thus, even as we speak of contracts, even as we consider what seems to be laid out in front of us, what seems apparent, what appears open to reading, to be read, one should remember the register of the unknown, the unknowable even, of the unreadable, of that which we did not sign up for, that we did not even know that we signed for, which affects us – regardless of how carefully, attentively, we attempt to read.

So, even as one reads, even as we – and here you are drawn into this contract, regardless of whether you asked for it or not, wanted to be or not – read, our attempt to attend to the text might well be haunted by the ghost of daddy; even whilst we can never be quite sure if the text, or we, are orphaned from its writer, its author, its *auctor*. Which means that even as we are attempting to attend to *Poetry from Beyond the Grave* we are never quite sure, we can never quite be certain, if we are reading the poems, the poets, the poems and poets through Chico Xavier, or "Chico Xavier." In other words – and here it is otherness that should be foregrounded – our writing, our inscription – and "our" here might well be indistinguishable from me, from I – of them, of the poems, the poets, of Chico, from Chico Xavier. Of whether Chico is our small, little, Xavier.

Which reopens the question that has been with us from the very beginning: *what is the premise of this response* to *Poetry from Beyond the Grave*? That is: what is promised at the end of all of this? Especially since this piece is coming at the end; especially since this has been premised as an afterword, a word that comes after – the last word, as it were.

Perhaps here, faced with the situation that all readings, all my writing on my readings – for I cannot claim any more than an interpretation, I cannot claim that I have even interpreted – are nothing more, and nothing less, than readings, all I can say is that this is a reading that stands after the word. Never forgetting Heraclitus' teaching in his opening fragment: that "the Word proves those first hearing it as numb to understanding as the ones who have not heard. Yet all things follow from the Word." (fragment of *Fragment 1*)[37] Thus, our task of attempting to read is – without even needing a transcendental conception of the word – potentially daunting: for, if we never quite know if we are even reading, that we have read, this suggests that not only are we potentially blind to our reading, we are always already blind in reading. Intimidating, quite possibly overwhelming even, as not only might we never quite know if we have read, nor if our readings are fraught with blindness, but that we might have read, might be reading, even if we are unaware of it, that we might be opening ourselves to the effects of, to being affected by, reading whilst we are blind to it.

However, we should also keep in mind that we can only see ghosts when we are not looking, when we are looking elsewhere, when we are blind.

Not that blindness and seeing are antonyms. For, as Amadeu – through Chico – teaches us: "The mystery of death is the mystery of life/ [...] That brings within, the dark, and opens the golden door / Of a world that amongst us is the unknown light."[38] Where not "death" and "life" are potentially intertwined, but that both remain "mysteries"; and the "light" – which is there, that much the poem makes clear to us – is "unknown." Which is why the "I" can only come "bearing witness" to the light – it is a testimony, nothing more and nothing else. Or, as Amaral Ornellas casts the "lofty quest" of the "lady of love": it is "thy quest of light."[39] A notion we see – allowing all possible ironies of a blind seeing to resound here – throughout *Poetry from Beyond the Grave*: in warnings ("those that from the light did not build their temples and dens/ Come down, with souls consumed"[40]); melancholic addresses ("it is not that I see this/ But it's sad"[41]); encouraging missives ("take sweet rest after toil / And bathe the heart in the light of life"[42]); thoughts of hope ("like a sublime song of hope / Over the brows of all who suffer / Yearning for more light, more freedom"[43]); and many others. Perhaps what we should bear in mind is the fact that even as "light" appears constantly, the fact that it continually shifts – continually remains a question even as we might embark on this quest of light with Ornellas' lady – reminds us that it remains, at least partially, shrouded in darkness, that we are, at least partially, veiled from it.

Thus, even as one is, I am, we are, attempting to read Chico Xavier's reading, writing, of the poets, their poetry, the poetry of others, it is an approach that never quite reaches, that never quite grasps, seizes, comprehends, that never quite even intends to fully apprehend. An approach that brings with it a simultaneous drawing back, drawing away, withdrawal; re-treat. And here, we might – perhaps even should – keep in mind Jean-Luc Nancy's reminder that to retreat is not just to back off, to keep a distance, admit a loss even, but to treat oneself again, to reopen a revisiting, an encountering that happens again.[44] Perhaps, at that very moment, without quite intending to, one may no longer be "numb" as those "first hearing it"; one might momentarily be opened to the possibilities of the word(s).

But since the "sun is new again, all day" (*Fragment 32*)[45] this suggests that we will, or at least might, never quite know whether we have understood, whether this second reading, re-reading, is a second first, or another reading; perhaps a reading that remains other to us. Thus, all understanding might well remain "numb to understanding."

Perhaps what Chico Xavier has foregrounded, the dossier that he opens, is that of one's relationality to reading itself. A relationality that resounds even, especially, when one is writing, particularly if one is writing as a response to another. This is the very register that Emmanuel opens in *Nosso Lar*, right at the beginning where we started. And here, we should bear in mind that Emmanuel is the one who signs off as the author of the preface to *Nosso Lar* – a description of the spirit Andre Luiz's journey; a spirit channelled through Chico Xavier – the same Emmanuel who is Xavier's spirit guide. Thus, in this encounter – Emmanuel's advice is directed to Luiz, or at least to Luiz's account, text – Chico is both the medium through which this is written, and also the one who calls forth the utterance from, through responding, to his guide. Hence, Emmanuel as guide, as father figure, is both called forth through the response, reading, of the little one, who at the same time is also the author of his guide, writer of the origin of this guidance by writing the guidance. That "real understanding and true love" go hand in hand, come together with, "anonymity." Not just in the sense of standing in the shadows, of being in the dark, and letting happen, but more precisely that at the point of the possibility of understanding, at the moment when love is possible, one is always anonymous, particularly to oneself, to one's self.

Where one is but a passage... a medium... where one is written upon as one is reading... as one is writing one's reading... and...

> ... in lieu of the 'subject', there is something like a place, a unique point of passage. It's like the writer for Blanchot: place of passage, of the emission of a voice which captures the "murmur" and detached itself from it, but which is never an 'author' in the classical sense...
>
> – Nancy[46]

Notes

1 Hélène Cixous, "'Mamãe, Disse Ele,' or Joyce's Second Hand," in *Stigmata*, trans Eric Prenowitz (London: Routledge, 2005), 135. And when we speak of stigmata, one should also open one's receptors to notions of stigmatisation, of what it means to be marked with a particular language – regardless of the fact that language comes before one – of how these citations, those that we have cited, inscribe themselves onto, into, us, become a part of us. Which might well be related to how we mark ourselves as one chooses what to say, what to cite – in citations, through citations, one might well already also stigmatise oneself.

2 Saint Augustine, *Confessions*, trans. Gary Wills (London: Penguin Books, 2006), 3.

3 *Genesis* 22.

4 Here, one might speculate on how Abraham's readiness to answer Yahweh's call had effects on the father-son relationship – of which nothing is spoken of, written; perhaps always shroud in darkness. However, one is almost certain that one paternal relationship was affected – momentarily effaced even – by the response to the call of another one.

5 *Matthew* 27:46.

6 Avital Ronell, *Dictations: On Haunted Writing* (Lincoln: University of Nebraska Press, 1993).

7 Here, one could also consider why the academic institution is so militant against plagiarism. Not just the blatant cases of cheating (where one is attempting to pass off, simulate, someone else's work for one's own) but even in the case where it is an honest error of never having before encountered that work that one is supposed to have copied from. Of course, one could argue that it is impossible to know the intent behind that act, and as such, one has to treat all cases of plagiarism, intentional or otherwise, as the same. The more interesting case is when one is accused of plagiarising oneself. Surely there, the notion of stealing another's idea can no longer be true: here, the crime, as it were, is economic in nature, in the precise sense that one's idea is owned by a particular home (*oikos*), in this case, a certain press. But even when it is a previously unpublished work, one can be called to task for failure to cite it, name it, label it.

One could posit that without the notation, it would be decontextualising the idea, pulling the idea out of time. However, one might also posit that the insistence on citing, citationality, serves to preserve the notion of originality: since every thing that is taken from elsewhere is cited, whatever that is not, is – by omission – original. In other words – and here it is most appropriate to foreground the otherness of words, of language itself – citationality protects the very possibility, illusion even, of authorship, of an author.

8 Avital Ronell, *Loser Sons: Politics and Authority* (Illinois: University of Illinois Press, 2012), 16.

9 In *A Man Called Love: Reading Xavier* (London: Capacete & Forlaget, 2010), Tamar Guimarães implies that Chico might have negotiated his complex relationship with the state – publishing rather left-wing, almost Socialist, positions whilst being a rather public figure in a military dictatorship run Brazil; being homosexual in a homophobic environment – by borrowing, speaking in and through, the voices of others. Guimarães posits that this might have allowed him to maintain a certain distance from his work, keep his writing persona and his person somewhat separate.

10 Herman Melville, *Bartleby the Scrivener: A Story of Wall Street* (New York: Melville House Publishing, 2004).

11 Clarice Lispector, *The Passion According to G.H.*, trans. Idra Novey (New York: New Directions Books, 2012), 22–3.

12 Martin Heidegger. "Only a God Can Save Us Now: An Interview with Martin Heidegger," trans. by David Schendler. *Graduate Faculty Philosophical Journal* 6.1 (Winter 1977): 6.

13 Avital Ronell, *The Telephone Book: Technology, Schizophrenia, Electric Speech* (Lincoln: University of Nebraska Press, 1989), 29.

14 Jacques Derrida, *Demeure: Fiction and Testimony*, trans. Elizabeth Rottenberg (Stanford: Stanford University Press, 2000), 83.

15 Giorgio Agamben, "What is the Contemporary?," in *Nudities*, trans. by David Kishik and Stefan Pedatella (Stanford: Stanford University Press, 2011), 13.

16 Francisco Cândido Xavier, *Nosso Lar – An Account of Life in a Spirit Colony in the World of Spirits* (Asa Norte: Conselho Espirita Internacional, 2006), 28.

17 Marshall McLuhan, *Understanding Media: The Extensions of Man* (New York: Mentor, 1964).

18 Marshall McLuhan and Quentin Fiore, *The Medium is the Massage: An Inventory of Effects* (London: Penguin Books, 1967).

19 Guimarães, *A Man Called Love*, 17.

20 Perhaps here, we could open the question of *whether one's own voice is always already heard from somewhere, elsewhere.* Can one really tell where the voice in one's head is coming from? And when we say *find your own voice* in relation to writing, does that not already imply that it is somewhere else to begin with, is not with one, and might never quite be found, be one's?

21 William Shakespeare, *Hamlet* (Washington DC: Folger Library Shakespeare, 2003), Act 1, sc. v. Emphasis mine.

22 Gilles Deleuze and Félix Guattari, *Kafka: Towards a Minor Literature*, trans. Dana Polan (Minneapolis: University of Minnesota Press, 1986), 16.

23 Ibid., 19.

24 Ibid., 21.

25 Ibid.

26 Ronell, *Loser Sons*, 156.

27 Avital Ronell, *Stupidity* (Chicago: University of Illinois Press, 2003), 287.

28 Radiohead. "Karma Police," on *OK Computer* (London: Parlophone Records, 1997).

29 Miguel de Cervantes, *Don Quixote*, trans. Walter Starkie (London: Signet Classic, 2001), 228.

30 Werner Hamacher, *Premises: Essays in Philosophy and Literature from Kant to Celan*, trans. Peter Fenves (Stanford: Stanford University Press, 1999), 129.

31 Ibid., 133.

32 Ibid.

33 Ibid.

34 Ibid., 137.

35 Ibid., 137–9.

36 Saint Augustine, *Confessions*, 153.

37 Heraclitus, *Fragments*, 3.

38 Amadeu, "The mystery of Death," this volume, 178.

39 Amaral Ornellas, "Ave Maria," this volume, 118.

40 Alvaro Teixeira de Macedo, "After the Party," this volume, 28.

41 Alfredo Nora, "Speedy Letter," this volume, 170. Emphasis mine.

42 Albérico Lobo, "From My Port," this volume, 166.

43 Fagundes Varela, "Immortality," this volume, 46.

44 I was first opened to this reading of "retreat" during Nancy's seminar – entitled *Art, Community, & Freedom* – at the European Graduate School, Saas-Fee, Switzerland in June 2006.

45 Heraclitus, *Fragments*, 21.

46 Jean-Luc Nancy. "An Interview with Jacques Derrida," *The Symptom* 10 (Spring 2009): http://www.lacan.com/thesymptom/?p=271

Contents

Translator's Note   5

Ignácio José de Alvarenga Peixoto
    Revived   16
    Redivivo   17
Souza Caldas
    Act of Contrition   22
    Ato de contrição   23
Álvaro Teixeira de Macedo
    After the Party   28
    Depois da festa   29
Casimiro de Abreu
    To My Land   30
    À minha terra   31
Castro Alves
    Let Us March!   36
    Marchemos!   37
Júlio Diniz
    Birds and Angels   44
    Aves e anjos   45
Fagundes Varela
    Immortality   46
    Imortalidade   47

Antero de Quental
- *To Death* — 56
- *À morte* — 57

Bittencourt Sampaio
- *To Mary* — 58
- *A Maria* — 59

João de Deus
- *Poetry from Beyond the Grave* — 60
- *Parnaso de Além-Túmulo* — 61

Lucindo Filho
- *No Shadows* — 62
- *Sem sombras* — 63

Luiz Guimarães Junior
- *Sonnet* — 64
- *Soneto* — 65

Cruz e Souza
- *Heaven* — 66
- *Céu* — 67

José Duro
- *To Men* — 68
- *Aos homens* — 69

Antônio Nobre
- *Sonnet* — 70
- *Soneto* — 71

Auta de Souza
- *Godspeed* — 72
- *Adeus* — 73

José do Patrocínio
  New Abolition   74
  Nova Abolição   75
Edmundo Xavier de Barros
  Faced with the Earth   76
  Diante da Terra   77
Artur Azevedo
  Miniatures of the Elegant Society   78
  Miniaturas da sociedade elegante   79
Cornélio Bastos
  Fear Not   84
  Não temas   85
Raimundo Correia
  Sonnets   86
  Sonetos   87
Casimiro Cunhia
  The Mistake   90
  O engano   91
Augusto dos Anjos
  Human Voice   92
  Voz humana   93
Batista Celepos
  Sonnets   94
  Sonetos   95
B. Lopes
  Heavenly Sightings   100
  Miragens celestes   101

Olavo Bilac
  Sonnet — 104
  Soneto — 105
Emílio de Menezes
  To My Friends on Earth — 106
  Aos meus amigos da Terra — 107
Luiz Pistarini
  In the Strange Portal — 108
  No estranho portal — 109
Alphonsus de Guimarãens
  To Believers — 110
  Aos crentes — 111
Guerra Junqueiro
  Eternal Victim — 112
  Eterna vítima — 113
Amaral Ornellas
  Ave Maria — 118
  Ave Maria — 119
Múcio Teixeira
  Honor to Work — 122
  Honra ao trabalho — 123
Raul de Leoni
  We… — 124
  Nós… — 125
Rodrigues de Abreu
  Saw Thee, Lord! — 126
  Vi-te, Senhor! — 127

Luís Murat
   Even Beyond...   130
   Além ainda...   131
Valado Rosas
   To My Brothers   132
   Aos meus irmãos   133
Hermes Fontes
   Sonnet   136
   Soneto   137
Juvenal Galeno
   From Here   138
   De cá   139
José Silvério Horta
   Prayer   144
   Oração   145
Cármen Cinira
   The Traveler and Faith   148
   O viajor e a Fé   149
Abel Gomes
   We Have Jesus   **150**
   Temos Jesus   **151**
Antônio Torres
   Ship of Dreams   152
   Esquife do sonho   153
Alberto de Oliveira
   Jesus   **154**
   Jesus   155

Belmiro Braga
   Verses from Another World   156
   Rimas de Outro Mundo   157
Gustavo Teixeira
   To Saint Peter of Piracicaba   162
   A São Pedro de Piracicaba   163
Pedro de Alcântra
   Page of Gratitude   164
   Página de gratidão   165
Albérico Lobo
   From My Port   166
   Do meu porto   167
Jesus Gonçalves
   Angel of Redemption   168
   Anjo de redenção   169
Alfredo Nora
   Speedy Letter   170
   Carta ligeira   171
Leôncio Correia
   Longing   174
   Saudade   175
A.G.
   Death   176
   Morte   177
Amadeu
   The Mystery of Death   178
   O mistério da morte   179

Alma Eros
   The Chalice   180
   O cálice   181
Marta
   Never Isolate Yourself   184
   Nunca te isoles   185
Unknown
   Meditating   188
   Meditando   189

Jeremy Fernando
   On Afterwords;
   or, What Comes After the Word...   193

www.ingramcontent.com/pod-product-compliance
Lightning Source LLC
Chambersburg PA
CBHW032126160426
43197CB00008B/536